Sex in
the Boardroom
Merydith Willoughby

Copyright © Merydith Willoughby 2024

All rights reserved. No part of this publication may be reproduced, distributed, or transmitted in any form or by any means, including photocopying, recording, or other electronic or mechanical methods, without the prior written permission of Merydith Willoughby, except in the case of brief quotations embodied in critical reviews and certain other non-commercial uses permitted by copyright law.

Willoughby, Merydith
SEX IN THE BOARDROOM

ISBN 978-0-9803741-1-7 (paperback)
ISBN 978-1-923214-06-4 (ebook)

While Merydith Willoughby has used her best efforts in preparing this book, she does not make any representation whether implied or otherwise about the accuracy or completeness of the contents of this book or the application of the book's contents to the reader's personal situation. The information and strategies contained in this book may not be suitable for your situation and no advice is given as to what you should or should not do in relation to what is written in this book whatsoever. Any resemblance to actual persons or events is coincidental.

First edition 2009
Second edition 2024

Leadership / Management

Merydith Willoughby
Executive advisor
https://lnkd.in/gigVsMPH
info@merydithwilloughby.com
New York City 718 790 9729
Australia 61 435086641

Contents

Merydith Willoughby.................................. vii

Introduction 1

Chapter 1 **Upline Upfront** 11

Chapter 2 **Square Peg** 23

Chapter 3 **Planning** 39

Chapter 4 **Everyone's Different**................ 53

Chapter 5 **Performance** 63

Chapter 6 **Your Style**................................. 79

Chapter 7 **Workplace Culture** 91

Chapter 8 **Thinking** 105

Chapter 9 **Continuous Improvement** 117

Chapter 10 **Keep it Simple** 129

Chapter 11 **Meetings** 143

Chapter 12 **Stress** 157

Chapter 13 **Ignorance is Bliss**............... 169

Chapter 14 **Fear**... 183

Chapter 15 **Fake it until You make it** 197

Chapter 16 **Bullying**.................................. 209

Chapter 17 **Holidays** 225

Chapter 18 **Globalisation** 239

Chapter 19 **The Long & Short of it**........ 255

Case Studies. 264
Glossary of Terms................................... 267

Merydith Willoughby

Merydith Willoughby is an international organisation development consultant with over two decades in this industry. Her strength is in seeing clarity when many are struggling with a complex situation that looms large in their consciousness. It is about making the impossible become possible by looking at it in a different way and then equipping people with the tools they need to help them proceed. She helps those she works with to take off their blinkers and be prepared to do things that were delayed because they hadn't understood the full implications.

Merydith has worked from boardrooms to the grass roots level of society. The approach used is based on keeping it simple, to focus on building competencies, to inform, involve and to engage all stakeholders. They then measure, monitor, mentor and manage key result areas. Used is a clear, systematic and practical approach with all clients and there is no guessing going on. The business signifies a great deal to Merydith and is an umbrella for many varied and inspiring activities.

Other books

If it's to be: It's up to me
Sex in the Boardroom
Thought Leadership
Back from Hell

There is something magnetic about watching a powerful leader in action. They start impressively and their whole performance indicates that they've done this before and they love it. The people listening to them are glued to their every word. They hardly breathe because they don't want to miss anything. They're smitten and they leave feeling alive, inspired and excited by what they've just been part of and want to do it again. It's an intimate experience. The speaker has charisma and it radiates in every direction. Groomed to perfection, they have perfected their body language. They know their topic and they deliver it very well using all of their assets. They are the Complete Package. Complete Packages exude energy and the audience wants to soak it up. Surely as a leader there would be nothing better than delivering a speech, chairing a meeting or holding a discussion and being treated like this because it means you are having an impact. Your message is getting across and people want to hear what you've got to say because what you say makes sense. It is up to you to be willing to review your style often and to change what needs changing. Actors do it all the time - so can you.

Introduction

Introduction

I was talking to an executive recently about *Sex in the Boardroom* and she remarked, "Sex *anywhere* would be good after having been single for five years."

True, I responded but it's actually not that sort of book. I told her it's a book to help leaders to look at what they're doing well and to identify the gaps. The process then assists them to implement strategies to be the type of leader they really want to be, not the one they've settled for. The book has been written for seasoned leaders and newer ones, I explained, because leaders are expected to perform on demand, to be able to create miracles when required and many are expected to be on call 24x7. They need the stamina of a bull and the hide of a rhinoceros.

Leaders can become addicted to the boardroom experience, the rush, the power, the heady sense of being the one in control. We spoke about this behaviour being fine in the short-term but how – in the long-term – it doesn't equate to being powerful or to the business operating optimally. Leaders need to learn how to maintain their powerful status, how to delegate effectively and they have to make sure that the right people are on their team.

Our conversation concluded by me telling my colleague that only then, when leaders have freed up all this energy, they might remember to get some of those powerful delights from somewhere outside the boardroom. My newfound friend acknowledged that this epitomises her experience as a leader and whilst her comment was flippant, that it still sounded like a good idea. This was obviously a lighthearted exchange but many truisms are said in jest.

Sex in the Boardroom has a systems approach to leadership development and it can be used as a tool to review what you are doing, to make minor changes or to make radical changes in the way you lead. Whatever your reason for working with the process, know that it can assist you to be powerful beyond belief *if* and only *if* you are willing to be honest with yourself and put in the hard yards.

Numerous books are written each year about the theoretical perspectives of leadership development yet few provide readers with key techniques, strategies to use or key questions to help them move out of the 'don't know what to do stage' to being powerful leaders in their own right. One without the other is not useful and many books just end up on the bookshelf collecting dust. Being a powerful leader doesn't just happen - it requires a lot of hard work, is time consuming and although some may have a natural tendency towards it, every leader has to continue to strive for excellence.

Many leaders become so focused on achieving business outcomes they don't even consider the possibility they need to change personal behaviours to keep themselves on top. If it does happen to cross their mind, they dismiss the thought as self-serving and a waste of time because they haven't discovered the key link between personal behaviour management and powerful leadership.

Some organisations realise they have to put the time and effort into developing their leaders because the so called level playing field has either gone or taken a beating with the increased competitiveness of the global market. Most organisations don't provide their leaders with enough – if any – development because they just expect them to know what to do. What development they do provide is usually 'training' as they don't know what else to look for or what else actually works. Training provides knowledge and gives participants information but it does not provide them with the strategies, guidance or support to change what is not working well in the workplace. Training also doesn't ask them the 'tough' questions that elicit insights. *Sex in the Boardroom* does. If you are willing to do the required work then this book can help you to be one of the leaders we talk about in the chapter, *Your Style* - which one is totally up to you.

SEX IN THE BOARDROOM

This book has humour throughout it because driving and developing the processes of leadership does not have to be hard, dry and boring. I want you to have a good laugh. We all know the role on any given day is anything between unrelenting and exhilarating and the more endorphins you have surfing in your body – the better. When you lead your people with a more playful attitude it can be infectious and resonate with everyone. This in turn helps create teams who are on *your* side and who feel passion, enthusiasm and excitement for what they are doing. No one wants to work with a powerful, yet cranky and unpleasant ole fart. Would *you*?

Leadership looks deceptively easy for on-lookers. They don't know how living in this pressure cooker environment for years undermines a leader being able to deliver ongoing sustainable outcomes. Sometimes you're on a high because everything is going so well, it all seems so effortless and then suddenly you think you're going nuts and losing the plot because things went pear shaped. You wonder why others can't see what is going on when it is blatantly obvious to you. And the big risk is burnout, with all that hard work going down the gurgler.

When organisations have unrealistic

expectations of their leaders and don't provide them with ongoing development it is unlikely that the business will operate optimally in the long-term. With leaders under constant pressure, when they're not taking time out to think, plan or to really clarify what they are doing and where these behaviours are not seen as a legitimate benefit, it's no wonder many fine businesses go down the tube. Get used to the idea that you don't have to work 24x7 to prove you are a successful leader. Learn how to work hard and smart. Identify what behaviours don't serve you well and change them, remembering to always bring it back to the bottom line: *if I do this, I will get this outcome for those I lead and for the organisation as a whole.*

As you might imagine it can bring huge financial and personal benefits to any organisation when they know and understand how to implement and work with systems and processes that deliver peak performance. When these structures are in place and adhered to the business gains many benefits.

You have to be action oriented and solution focused. You can't let personal flaws, nervousness or self doubts get in the way. And because of this, it is clear the most exciting time an executive has is often in the *boardroom* because they're firing on all cylinders, they are respected, listened to and exalted because they lead the show, are in control, are powerful, knowledgeable and commanding. You're *hot*, damn hot and it feels *good*.

There is a compelling and heady feeling associated with being powerful and with other things we experience and desire in our life – great sex being right up-there. And if we agree that most of us want to experience this feeling over and over again, then the boardroom is often the closest to it that many leaders get because of the incredible demands on them to perform at such a high level day after day, year after year.

Naturally after a time, being this important to so many people can go to one's head. Being completely focused on the job at hand means the situation can become addictive, even though there's no consciousness of an addiction developing. Feeling important is like an aphrodisiac experience, giving a rush, a sense of pleasure and confidence and a desire for more of whatever it is that feels so good.

The energy required to keep operating at the top can be mentally *and* physically exhausting. Unless you implement strategies to maintain it, chinks in the armour could appear when you least expect it (or least need it) and then your once powerful leadership status might become mediocre and something you only remember in your dreams. As for those certain *other* areas of your life that also deliver the sought-after feelings of excitement and satisfaction, where you also want to perform with considerable expertise and want to be considered a powerful and exciting force. Well, they are much less likely to be the way you would like them when you have so much on your plate. Or perhaps they don't exist at all. By the time you get home at night, who cares about the other great delights in life when what you really need right now is to go to bed and sleep.

Chapter 1
Upline Upfront

Chapter 1 Upline Upfront

Regardless of your level of seniority in the workplace, you will be accountable to someone. Every manager has key people to whom they have to answer. To meet or exceed expectations, you must have a working relationship with all of your stakeholders.

It is common for workers at any level to be too scared to tell the plain truth to their manager. They would rather say what they think you want to hear, or place an emphasis on what's going well, either missing or bypassing the things that you need to know to do your job effectively. They may have worked in situations where the truth wasn't valued, where their honesty was not welcome and their suggestions had no impact on anything. Afraid or disempowered, the incentive is to cover their backside at any cost – it is not safe to reveal themselves or to be the bearer of bad news.

Fear isn't the only thing that influences the information you get. Politics can play heavily in any workplace: untruths told, information withheld and games played in order to win a point. While a little competition can be healthy, this game playing can bring you unstuck if you don't play smart, don't know who to trust or if you're unaware you're actually part of the game.

You can't afford to be kept in the dark and

SEX IN THE BOARDROOM

taken by surprise. You must be completely sure that your people share all relevant information with you, that it is accurate and that you really know what is happening in your area of responsibility. Without this certainty, you cannot confidently make decisions that affect the bottom line and the viability of your business.

Case study

In regular meetings with her new line manager (which were often cancelled due to his commitments as a senior executive), Chris was reluctant to raise a problem she was grappling with. She hoped that time would resolve the dilemma and her feelings of inadequacy about her new management role. She hoped she would soon impress her boss with the performance and results she and her team would achieve. She was sure she could get things on-track without bothering him, getting him angry or giving him reason to doubt her abilities.

The situation continued for months, causing her anxiety and sleepless nights. Try as she might, she could not solve the problem by herself. Chris reported the success stories and progress on her plans to get the projects successfully completed. From her manager's perspective, all projects were on time, on task and meeting Key Performance Indicators (KPIs).

Chris is not generally a dishonest person. She was not withholding information because she wanted to – she just didn't know what to do or how to do it. Chris was following the 'head in the sand principle' of management, hoping that if she ignored it, it would go away and somehow fix itself. She hadn't stopped to think about the consequences of what she was doing, the impact that it would have on everyone involved and in particular, on herself and her manager.

Eventually Chris had to tell her manager what was really happening because all was about to be revealed anyway.

Challenge it

Don't follow the head in the sand principle. Withholding information is not fair on your line manager and it is not fair on you. Your line manager bears responsibility and may be hauled over the coals for the choices you make and the information you conceal. Small problems that could easily be fixed – if the manager knows about them – can quickly escalate and spiral out of control.

Your choice to delay addressing issues can sap your energy, make you worry needlessly about problems that don't exist, create new problems or make up a million reasons to rationalise why you are right to keep avoiding the situation. You risk being labelled as inept, being sacked, or helping to create the nightmare that you were trying so hard to avoid in the first place. No one is perfect and as leaders, we are always learning. It is much better to confront your fear head-on: tell your manager exactly what is happening and be solution focused. Say what you intend to do about it and if necessary ask for help from the right people.

Workplace dilemma

Tony was a team leader. He was keen for a new role with more responsibility. However, his own performance and that of his team wasn't strong and it wasn't helping that he was bored, having been in the position for a long time.

He was supposed to have weekly meetings with his manager but she was too often unavailable. She was always busy with other issues and focused on what she needed to do to meet her own manager's objectives and corporate benchmarks. When he informed her about what he needed help with through the official channels it took her over a week to respond by which time other issues had to be dealt with. Nothing was being resolved – issues were piling up on top of each other.

Tony was frustrated with her and felt powerless because he was not getting the support he needed to perform his role effectively. His manager seemed to have no idea about the impact that her behaviour was having on him and his team. He felt she put too much pressure on him with time management and report writing when there were so many other influences that created situations he was supposed to fix.

And now, he has been given an ultimatum. For the second time he hadn't met his performance criteria and if he didn't improve, he may be sacked. This caused him great angst as he had been with the organisation for a long time, he had a mortgage on his house, had recently married and he had to care for a dependant adolescent son.

Through our sessions, Tony became to understand that he was part of the problem and to resolve the issues he needed to change. When we discussed what he could do to get back on-track, Tony was scared stiff, but he was willing to take the risk because the way things were going, he would be lucky to have his job in six months time.

What Tony learned
- He must learn how to manage his manager.
- He must be honest with himself.
- He must be honest with his manager about his needs.
- Managers have their own workload and

they depend on their team to do their own job.
- His manager isn't following the 'read my mind' model of management. He simply needs him to articulate his concerns. If he wants to wait for his manager to read his mind then he must be prepared to wait for a long time.
- His manager has her own manager and the chain of command goes on and on.
- He must be honest with his manager and stop pretending things are okay.
- He must stop blaming her for his lack of courage.
- He does indeed have power and he can't continue to whinge if he isn't prepared to act.
- When he manages his manager, it becomes easier to manage his team because he is then able to lead his team with confidence and clarity.
- When he treats his team with respect, his team responds positively. When he must reprimand them, he does so with respect and with clarity, so they know what they need to do to correct the problem.

After his commitment to change and his hard work, which he found quite challenging at times, Tony became part of his organisation's high performance culture. He now feels proud that he was able to turn around a potentially disastrous situation and delighted that he learnt how to manage his manager and to lead his team powerfully. Tony knows he can face his fears and challenges, that he can enjoy having powerful people on his team and that he needs to have someone external on his side who provides him with 'another pair of eyes', support, encouragement and who is willing to ask him the tough questions that empower him to be courageous in his role.

Summary

Once you're in a leadership position you will realise just how vital it is to be totally honest in the workplace. If you don't have all the information it's like having flat batteries in your torch: you are leading your people in the dark. You will have to work out ways of getting all of the information you need to do your role effectively. Don't assume that you are getting it because history shows clearly that it doesn't happen because fear of looking stupid affects most of us and any normal person doesn't want to put themselves in that position any more than

SEX IN THE BOARDROOM

is necessary. Either way - withholding information from your manager or your people withholding it from you doesn't help you to achieve successful business outcomes because you're only ever leading with dead batteries or no batteries at all. Working 'in the dark' potentially costs industry significantly through lost productivity and profitability, not to mention the human costs in stress and anxiety.

Concealing facts from key people may be systemic in organisations, going right up the chain of command. Always remember that you need to set an example for your people. You don't want your staff to do it to you, so don't do it yourself. So be upfront about it. *Everyone* needs to know that you don't want to do it in the dark. You want and need the lights ON.

Questions

1. Have you ever withheld information from your manager?
2. Do you hope problems will go away so that you don't have to address them?
3. Are all of your people clear about what you want and need to do your job effectively?
4. Are the communication channels open?
5. Do you provide regular, constructive feedback to those you lead and to colleagues?
6. Do you ask your team if they have enough information to do their job effectively?
7. Do you always show respect to your people?
8. Do you pay attention and scrutinise your own actions and motives?
9. Are you aware of how (or if) you sabotage your relationship with your manager?
10. How can you circumvent issues before they escalate?

Chapter 2
Square Peg

As a leader, the pressures you face are unlikely to subside and your top priority must be to do the things that will make your role easier. One simple but important way you can do this is to spend the time necessary to get the right people on your team and in your organisation in the first place – not down the track when issues are emerging.

The process of employing the right people is no small feat and it is inevitable you will at times wish you hadn't hired a particular employee. When people are not aligned to your business, regardless of how terrific they might be, they will not help you to achieve your organisational goals.

Gently does it

We've all seen it. The *we have a vacancy so let's fill it* mentality that dominates when managers are under pressure. We rush, we take shortcuts, we hire someone – anyone – quickly. And we've all seen the results of it. We pay the price. The wrong person is hired. We find ourselves looking for a replacement for someone who didn't stay long or we're stuck with problems of a mismatch, under-performance, conflict. None of these scenarios makes it easy for you to do your job effectively.

So put more effort into the hiring process. Do everything possible to know that you're making a decision you're not going to regret. Don't worry if it takes longer, because research shows that you will probably save yourself many headaches and significant sums of money in the long run.

Take as much time as you need when choosing candidates to interview. What type of person are you looking for? Identify what skills and experience you need in an employee for the current position but be just as clear on the characteristics you want to avoid. Is the person a good fit with your other people? How is this person going to help you to meet your business objectives?

CVs

CVs aren't gospel. They're *supposed* to be gospel, since they are a legal document but a number of studies back our suspicions that candidates don't always tell the whole truth when they prepare their CV. And alas, it seems that the higher the position the more you will need to validate the details, so read the CV closely. If the candidate interests you, independently confirm their details. And go on your gut feeling, because sometimes that is going to be the only warning that you are about to hire a square peg.

Chapter 2 Square Peg

Outsourcing

More and more organisations are outsourcing recruitment. It is primarily done because of a lack of time and a belief that recruitment organisations are experts in the area but it does not guarantee you will get a better quality of candidate. Many square pegs make it through.

The recruitment organisations may hear what you want but they don't know what your culture is like, the daily pressures you face and they don't know the other members of the team with whom this candidate will have to work.

You, the leader, will *always* be the one who must work with the person, so in the best interests of yourself and your team, be involved in the whole process. Don't think you're too busy. You're not too busy to identify the right person to help you get less busy. Even when the recruitment organisation informs you they have found the right person, don't stop there, get to know the person. Just how well you need to get to know them will depend on the level they will be in the organisation. The higher their new position is to be, the greater the need to get to know them very well before you make the final decision to sign that legally binding contract.

SEX IN THE BOARDROOM

Honeymoon period

Most people can learn how to write a CV and learn how to behave in an interview. They can learn to say what needs to be said in order to be seen in a favourable light. And if they get the job, there will be a period where even a square peg will be on their best behaviour. During this honeymoon period, workplace harmony is high, there are no major crises and productivity is at a level that is sustainable. As the square peg becomes more comfortable, more at ease and more able to be true to their character, things change. At this critical juncture, if you don't manage the situation well, the culture and the rest of the team may take a hammering and your pleasant surroundings may disintegrate into bitchiness, gossiping, bullying and other unsavoury behaviours. This is not so different to the way kids act out in the playground. Be aware of it and don't let it happen to you. You often spend more time with work colleagues than you do with your own family and anyone who associates with people for hours at a time knows what issues they can face.

Mistakes

It's worth investing a lot of time to get the hiring process right in the first place and not thinking down the track that I hired the wrong person and won't say anything because it'll work out in the end and I don't want to upset anyone.

That said, there is always a chance you may hire the wrong person regardless of how much effort you put in to find the right one – but there is a lot that you can do to give yourself the best possible chance. The questions at the end of this chapter will help you to understand why it is worth putting time in right at the start rather than trying to fix it once they've been hired. It will also help you understand the real cost to you, your team and the whole organisation in qualitative and quantitative terms.

Personality vs skills

I have noticed a move by some organisations to spend the time to find the right person who has the right personality but not necessarily all of the skills. They are willing to hire a person who may not have all of the required attributes but will complement the culture, will fit into their way of doing things and will share their core values and principles. They recognise that they can upgrade the person's skills but not their personality or character. They have learnt the hard way that people are not monkeys – you can't just train them and expect them to behave in a certain way because the human personality is powerful and is always expressing itself. They

SEX IN THE BOARDROOM

acknowledge that human foibles are real and they want to minimise the impact as much as possible so that they can get on with doing the job they've been paid to do rather than spending inordinate amounts of time managing drama and problems in the workplace.

Case study

Colin is the manager of his own business. He is a switched-on leader who has been involved in many different areas of business over many years, so he genuinely understands it well. His organisation is successful and continues to expand.

He is constantly frustrated because employees leave him after he has spent significant time training them. It costs him dearly in terms of his time, other business activities and the general annoyance of always having to train new employees. It stops him from being able to pursue other business opportunities. It stops him from being the outstanding Chief Executive Officer (CEO) and entrepreneur that he is.

The problem is that Colin always thinks in terms of long-term relationships and he tends to assume that his employees will as well. He has never really taken the time to sit and think about what he is doing to create the problem in the first place by hiring the wrong employees.

He is also frustrated because he feels they rely on him too much and don't use their own skills to answer queries and follow up with their clients' needs.

Colin feels that you sometimes get lucky and find fantastic employees and you just have to put up with the others. While he recognises that the difficult ones take up too much of his time, he doesn't know how to change the situation. He is wasting more and more time doing work that shouldn't be part of his duties, so his personal productivity is being seriously compromised through working in the business instead of on it.

It has now become clear to Colin that he must put more time into getting the right people and he must specifically ask them what they seek from the position. By finding out if they fit his criteria, he sees what the employee offers him rather than making himself fit in with what they want.

Yep – this is The One

Does this sound familiar to you?

You've read the CV. You've spent time with the candidate. You're sure that this is the right person for the job to be done. Well okay, so you haven't spent *quite* as much time as you should have finding out about this person because you don't have the time, but well, they seem okay and they've said the right things and well, yes, the CV looks good enough. Great job, well done. The organisation and new person can now live happily ever after.

Is this your experience? We'd all love to be part of this fairy tale but odds are there's going to be some person ready to turn your world upside down. It won't be long until you're wondering what on earth is going on.

When you're willing to put the time in to get the *right* employees, you'll notice that time spent in the negotiating stage pays dividends. You'll also notice that you might not get it right every time but you do the best you can and you will start to get better at spotting the square pegs before you hire them. The point is to recognise that you can train someone but it is difficult or impossible to change someone's belief system and attitude unless that person is committed to the process and works hard to change what they don't like about themselves.

Don't give up straight away

It's not unusual for someone to appear unsuitable for their job initially even though they could actually be quite good at it after you've given them some development (well, maybe a lot). People can adapt, job descriptions change. So above all, be flexible. People can surprise you and sometimes they just need the opportunity.

Each person will be different and will bring different things to the team. They may not be the same as you or think the same way but they still produce the outcomes that you want and need. If this situation occurs then it's more about you and it's best to learn how to live with their peculiarities. Don't fall into the habit of only being able to work with people who have your personality because you will miss many opportunities to learn from each other.

When you've tried everything and the square peg just has to go

I've never worked with a manager who found 'getting rid' of people to be easy or something that gave them great pleasure. Many spend months or years putting it off rather than doing it. Only the brute managers have no feelings on this one. Most struggle with it and can stay awake for a few nights planning the best way to execute it, worry after they've done it and are really concerned about how the person is coping. However sometimes you have to do it not just because of redundancies, amalgamations or other necessary changes to the workplace but because the square pegs don't fit in, they don't want to or simply can't.

People can usually tell if they are a square peg and it can be liberating to get the push they need to do something to which they are more suited. Once the initial shock has passed, many people who have been 'managed out' from their current position say that although it was traumatic at first, it turned out to be the best thing that could have happened to them.

Each industry and country is different and it is important to have legal advice to ensure you never face an unfair dismissal case.

Exit interviews

Resist the temptation to skip an exit interview because you are feeling stressed or are time-poor. These interviews are worthwhile for the chance to learn something from someone else's experience that can be useful for future reference. That said; keep in mind that sometimes fear may influence the type of information given.

Prepare for this meeting; know what the person leaving will be given in terms of remuneration. Take the time and effort to find out from the employee involved what they would like for an outcome and why this is so. Ask what they believe has led to this situation and how they may have contributed to it.

Look at your organisation's policy and follow it to the letter but add your humanity into the meeting. When people are sacked or retrenched, you need to expect a certain level of animosity towards you and the organisation because of the uncertainty they feel about what the future now holds for them. They will be concerned about a range of issues including the impact on their family, future job prospects, financial position and more.

Compassion is the key in this situation and always remember that in another time and place it could be you who is on the receiving end. And never, ever deliver this message via an email, telephone call, SMS, through the grapevine or through someone else. It is your responsibility and you need to have the courage to do it.

Summary

You're a leader, so pressure is never going to just go away. Having the right team in place means you are better placed to respond appropriately to that pressure, instead of buckling under it.

Think about how much of your time a functioning team takes on a daily basis even when they fit in with the organisational plan. Then think about the price you pay in stress, drama and conflict when you have the wrong people on your team. It won't be hard to see it's worth putting in the extra time to find the right people because it is just too expensive to make mistakes.

Hiring the right people with the right personality certainly doesn't mean you are clones of each other.

It means that you know what you want, you have identified what your culture is and you know the people who will enhance it to help you to go from strength to strength.

SEX IN THE BOARDROOM

Questions
1. Have you ever employed someone who fits the profile of a square peg?
2. What was the real cost in terms to you and your people?
3. How much time did you spend trying to help the person to fit in?
4. How much of your own productivity did you lose by doing that?
5. How much time did the situation take that should have been spent with other people and on other tasks?
6. How did the square peg affect your morale and that of your team?
7. What were the key things you noticed about these employees compared to someone who does fit in?
8. How long did it take you to realise that someone was a square peg?
9. What did you do about it?
10. How can you identify someone who isn't right before you hire them?

Chapter 3
Planning

Chapter 3 Planning

Oops. Another day, another week, another month, another year has somehow slipped by, laments those who don't plan. Don't let this be you.

Imagine that someone invites you over for dinner. They want to get to know you better because you've clicked. They tell you the name of their suburb but they don't tell you their address, even though you've not been there before and won't be able to find it without a few clues. What would you think? Would it seem a little strange to you? Of course it is, but no more absurd than not planning for business success.

Failing to plan leaves every member of the organisation in a state of confusion and uncertainty, each wondering what is going on and why everyone else knows what is going on when they certainly don't. They don't dare ask because they're worried about revealing their ignorance.

Being prepared for action
If planning is so important to leaders and makes such a difference to organisational success then why do so few do it and why do most of us avoid it like the plague? The answer is simple. It takes time. You have to stop and think. Most of us would rather jump into action straight away because we

haven't been taught how to plan, don't understand the importance of it or we see no real purpose to doing it.

If we choose to bypass this most important component of success, if we don't spend time in vision, we'll end up stuck in the problems and lost in the drama of situations. The result? Not surprisingly, we end up getting more of what we've always had. We feel frustrated and blame anything but our own refusal to do what works and works well.

Planning – *quality* planning – is crucial to organisational success. When planning is prioritised, organisations can thrive. At *any* given point, you should know exactly where you are with your business development, have a plan for your short-term and long-term goals in your mind and down on paper.

When you're doing something without a plan you effectively put yourself and other participants in the same situation: in a metaphorical car, preparing to go somewhere and although you know the rough direction, the details are sketchy at best.

As a leader you would be wise to understand that it's up to you. You can get help, you can delegate, you can have the best people on your team but at the end of the day, it'll be your head on the plate if you don't get it right. You are the only one who can change what you don't like. You need to have the discipline of a monk and be incredibly focused. You won't be alone if you think planning is just another task to be done but you can change this and know that planning should be as important to you as food is to your survival. If you are not planning to be successful then ultimately you are planning to fail.

Daily planning
It is important to take the time to write things down, to consolidate and to plan what will secure the maximum benefit. You can develop a process where you put planning at the top of your agenda, showing your commitment to achieving excellence and to doing the best you can do with the resources you have. It doesn't mean every day will be a bed of roses or that all targets will be met. It means you will spend 10 minutes at the beginning of the day working out what you need to do and identifying what you have accomplished, what needs to be rescheduled and what doesn't need to be done at all.

The process of writing a daily To Do list helps clarify priorities. It takes the emotion out of it and provides something tangible to which you can regularly refer. Many people write their lists down on little bits of paper, lose them and keep writing new ones – it's not a winning system. Use your workbook.

Initially, some leaders find their To Do list is very long. They see everything on it as urgent, that there are conflicting priorities and it is hard to know which one to do first. So be realistic when writing your list and remember there are only so many hours in a day. Always keep some free time for unexpected things.

Remember to *use* your list. Learn to differentiate between urgent, very important, important and not at all important. Most of us are stuck in urgent and when you think about it, very few things are urgent. Some are very important but most things just have to be done. Many things don't ever have to be done and it's fantastic to be able to look at a list and realise that a number of things can be given the flick. A sense of relief comes over you when you get to this stage and you just focus on the things that will make a huge difference and that are necessary. You also learn to delegate and this is another moment of glory. Racing mindlessly from one thing to the next can become a thing of the past.

Each day look over your To Do list from the previous day and tick off what you've completed.

Assess what is left undone and if something really does need to be done put it on today's list. Decide if there are things that don't need to be done at all and take great pleasure to write *no* beside them. Saying *no* can remind you that you are in the driver's seat rather than being driven by everyone else.

Weekly planning

Diarise a meeting with yourself each week. Prise yourself away from your desk - go somewhere where you will be undisturbed, where you will feel relaxed and where you will enjoy the time. Schedule it for the time of the day you feel your best. Mornings seem to work best because you can get on with the rest of your day and there is less risk of your meeting being passed over for something else. There is *nothing* more important than you taking time out to plan for your success. Put this information in your workbook and follow an agenda just as you do for any meeting. Think long and hard about what you're doing as a leader, what you need to be doing and how you can achieve these goals. But the most important thing for you to do right now is to get into the habit of having your weekly meeting.

My clients say that this is the single most important thing they ever do. Remember bad habits are easy to get into – good habits take a little longer

SEX IN THE BOARDROOM

to become normal for you and are easily lost in times of stress. Keep this habit though because it's a good one.

Mini project
Planning for 12 months
1. Write a plan for 12 months. Schedule a half a day to do it and maybe do it on the weekend where you can be in your tracksuit, glass of wine in one hand and pen in the other, where you are very relaxed and won't be disturbed. This could be a solo activity or you could have a couple of trusted colleagues with you. It can be a good brainstorming opportunity. In this instance, detail is good as it frees you to become creative and to think laterally. Observe the process, see how effective it is for you and think how you can improve it.
2. Get excited about your business plan and goals and put what you'd actually love to achieve, rather than what you have to achieve. You can fine-tune it later. Divide the plan into categories and include all of the necessary information.
3. Hold yourself accountable for what you

write down - everything needs to be realistic, manageable and achievable. This is where you have to be tough on yourself. There are no acceptable excuses for not doing what you have said you'll do, so think carefully before you commit to anything.

4. Once you have everything written down, think about how it fits into your three month schedule and then reduce it further to one month. All plans must fit together and be cohesive.

5. The final step is to condense it further, take time to think how your weekly and daily activities fit into your long-term goals and make mental notes as to how everything fits together and how you'll manage it. Write this information in your workbook. And then get into action to create this fantastic plan, check in regularly to see how you're going, identify the results you've got from working with this process and see how your behaviour and attitude to what you do changes as you achieve your goals and plans.

Like any leader, you will wear a number of hats, so

it is important to avoid taking on so much that you are unable to achieve your desired outcomes. Think about the following. How do you manage to stay on-track? How do you manage to say no to people? How tough is it? How wonderful and liberating is it? How do you know you're doing what you need to be doing? You should commit to this rigorous process every 12 months to see just how effective your systems and processes really are.

If this process is likely to be put in the too hard basket then get someone to work with you and to teach you how to do it. It is not something to be bypassed. Once you are in the habit of planning and can see the significant benefits for having persisted with it, you can roll it out across the whole organisation. Imagine a business where people are focused, clear about their next step and don't waste time on peripheral issues – it sounds like heaven to me.

Plans with benefits

Initially, planning is a time consuming process. It is avoided because we see it as time spent, instead of time invested. This is an important difference.

Effective planning provides leaders with strategies that will save significant time and bring benefits to the business that should not be underestimated. Effort is directed to things that increase productivity and profitability, leaders learn what does and doesn't work and less time is wasted on things that are not of strategic benefit to the company. A few of the benefits include - adopting new ways of thinking and behaving, implementing effective systems and processes, become action oriented and solution focused. All of these contribute significantly to increased organisational strength.

Good planning does not guarantee smooth sailing but once leaders see what a huge difference it makes they wonder why they didn't commit to the process earlier. The benefit to the business' overall profitability cannot be over-emphasised and after all, that's why we're all in business.

Summary
When you have clear business goals for the next 12 months entrenched in your mind and committed to writing, link them with every business decision you make, every single day. In this way you can take your business to heights you've only ever dreamt of because you know at any given time how a decision you are about to make will benefit the business goals.

Effective planning and review help to keep you in touch with the big picture and ensures you are developing strategies and actions to achieve your organisational goals. Without planning you're just adrift hoping that things will go right and determinedly ignoring the fact that you may well wash up somewhere you don't want to be.

In the long-term, planning helps you to stay sane, to focus on what will make the biggest difference to you, your organisation and to those you lead. You will become much more confident about your ability and will surround yourself with people who help you to achieve your business outcomes. You learn that you can't do it all yourself and that you don't want to. You have people who are just as good as you are (or better) who can handle much of what you thought you should be doing. So you learn to delegate and learn how to say *no*. You and those you lead waste much less time on activities that are not adding value to your business, fire fighting in problem areas and being caught in dramas. Your time in the planning process – in visioning – is time very well invested.

Questions

1. When was the last time you sat down and really thought about what you're doing?
2. When was the last time you sat down and really thought about what you're achieving?
3. When was the last time you sat down and really thought about what you need to achieve?
4. What are your key objectives for the short-term?
5. What are your key objectives for the long-term?
6. Do you have regular briefings with your staff?
7. Do you take the time necessary to think about setting clear goals for the organisation?
8. Do you have a clear one month, three month, 12 month plan?
9. Do you link everything you do each day to that 12 month plan to ensure you are meeting organisational goals and objectives?
10. Who do you need to help you achieve your outcomes?

Chapter 4
Everyone's Different

Chapter 4 Everyone's Different

We know it, we see it every day and scientists can now prove it. People are different. So why is it that in business we expect people to behave the same? Why is it that we are surprised when an approach which works with one person is a disaster with someone else? Why aren't differences taken into account and different learning styles acknowledged?

This makes the leader's role even more important in the workplace. Although we have a modus operandi and sometimes slip into the assumption that everyone thinks like us, as leaders we must see through this. We must remain conscious of the fact that everyone is very different, that they think differently about situations and they act differently when put under the same stress.

Where does this leave a leader? Well, armed with this information, we as leaders get insights into human behaviour and can learn how to get the best out of those we lead. In the first instance it may make our role harder and at times confusing but in the long-term it becomes much easier because we know the strengths and weaknesses that our people have and can work within those constraints. Each person we work with will have their own best style of performing. If we can identify this, we will benefit significantly.

These differences can actually be advantageous. In any team, it is best to have people who think quite differently, to give yourself the best chance of achieving a high performance. To have a fully functioning team, it's important to invest the time to get the right people into the right roles. However, with all the benefits that this diversity within the team can bring, comes the potential for friction and misunderstandings.

How do you as a leader learn what's going to work for each of your employees? The answer is *observation*. Take out time to listen to them and be clear when communicating what you need them to do. And then observe some more.

Differences come with the extent to which you have to direct someone. One person may appreciate comprehensive and clear directions while another may feel resentment that their initiative is unrecognised, their experience unvalued and their judgment questioned. You will need to work out who appreciates micro management and who does not. The more experienced and senior people are, the less they want and need micro managing.

As leaders we need to understand a certain amount about the psychology of human behaviour. Much information abounds in this field and you would be wise to study some of it.

Chapter 4 Everyone's Different

Case study

We have a team of four where each of us is and capable high achievers but with very different styles, ways of doing things, ways of thinking and processing information.

One of the team is extremely intolerant of these differences. If the four of us are at the table with different ideas, she sees it as a bother because she has to go to the trouble of telling us why we are wrong and she is right. I'm the opposite – I love the different ideas and if we are all thinking the same way I worry what important information or ideas we're missing.

I pointed out that having four independent minds is a strength not a weakness and that perhaps we do a course on valuing our differences. That way we can learn how to get the most out of our respective strengths and by understanding each other we could work more easily together.

But no. *We don't need to do a course*, she said. *You just have to be more like me.* Julia

Emotional intelligence

The concept of emotional intelligence was popularised by Daniel Goleman in the 1980s to explain differences in how people interact and form relationships with others. For many this has proved to be a valuable concept that is worth understanding.

SEX IN THE BOARDROOM

Human beings are complicated and the more you understand about their behaviour the better.

Some people think that there is only one form of intelligence and it can be measured in an IQ test whilst other people believe there are many forms of intelligence. Your workplace will reflect this same diversity. There will be some employees who are very easy to get on with and there will be some who drive you crazy because they seem to put a spanner in the works at every step.

The following case study identifies an employee who was brilliant – the sort of person who is a pleasure to manage, always works hard and has the organisation's interests at heart. He is also a team person and gets on with most people. Everyone will at times throughout their working life make mistakes and it will be out of character for them to respond in the way they do. When they are a valued employee, you are likely to make exceptions for them and help them to overcome their dilemmas because the business needs to keep them.

Situation

A morning shift employee went home without reporting a safety breach. When the situation blew up an hour into the afternoon manager's shift, he was annoyed and embarrassed to be in the dark about a serious safety breach and thought that any disciplinary action the employee got would be richly deserved. After calming down a little and reading the records from the morning shift, it became immediately obvious that no attempt had been made to cover it up. Concerned that an employee with a good record had placed himself in a difficult position, the manager telephoned him at home and strongly advised him to report back to work and make a clean breast of the situation. During the conversation it became clear that the employee had been badly rattled by what happened and had gone home without saying anything simply because he didn't know what to do and was afraid of the consequences. However the strict regulations to which the organisation was bound required that the employee report the breach before leaving the site. Because of the afternoon shift manager's action, the employee got the opportunity to minimise the damage he did to his career and reputation. By the time the CEO arrived in the control centre to check on what had happened the person responsible for the breach was at a desk writing out a full report. He was still severely reprimanded but kept his job. The organisation kept its valuable employee and was in fact improved by the experience. Dale

SEX IN THE BOARDROOM

Another perspective

This particular shift manager is a colleague of mine and he put his job on the line by contacting the employee at home. Had he been found out, his job as well as that of the employee would have been on the line. He knew the employee concerned, realised how anxious and upset he would be and suspected that there must be a good reason why he had gone home without writing a report or advising the shift manager.

I'm not advocating anything here – as a leader there will be many times when you have to make a decision based on the information you have at hand. When deciding on your own actions, you will need to be aware of the potential penalty that an exceptional employee might pay because of panicking because of being frightened and uncertain about what to do. You also need to be aware of the potential penalties for your own actions if you do something that is not an accepted practice in your workplace. Dale

CEO's perspective

This organisation had a large number of stakeholders. The board treats its responsibilities seriously and expects the highest standards of performance and responsibility from the CEO.

Like every CEO he wanted the organisation to

Chapter 4 Everyone's Different

run smoothly and all his staff to be happy but he had some uncompromising aspects to his personality. In particular he did not place a particularly high value on the skills of lower and middle level staff with the result that staff turnover had increased and the sanction of dismissal for making mistakes was always uppermost in his mind. However being a realist, he was aware that this course of action would not be followed without exception.

When alerted by the shift manager to the safety breach that had occurred, he proceeded immediately to the control centre to conduct his own investigation. He tried to keep an open mind, but tense over the constant pressure from the board, he became incensed that an apparent staffing incompetence had jeopardised his plans. After investigating the situation, he made the decision to reprimand the employee, not sack him. The most important reason for this was the fact that the employee had not attempted to hide his mistake and had made a full report including everything that he had done wrong himself, making no attempt to have post incident justification. Dale

SEX IN THE BOARDROOM

Summary

Call it what you want – emotional intelligence, social functioning, knowing how to behave with other people – it doesn't matter because the impact is the same. Some people are easy to manage while others will drive you to despair. It's up to you to manage all of the people effectively, not just some and it may be in your best interests to understand the concept of emotional intelligence because it has some great tips on human behaviour and how to get the most out of your people. It also helps to have a term to call it because then colleagues know what you're discussing and it gives you a framework to work within. Whilst it's not your responsibility to educate those you lead about this subject, a wise manager will do just that because they know by educating people in this area that their job will be made a whole lot easier and when that happens and you have a high functioning team, productivity and profitability reflect it.

Chapter 5
Performance

Chapter 5 Performance

Thousands of performance management models have been developed since the Industrial Revolution. Business leaders are constantly told the *best* way to do things, the *new* way to manage people, the *new* way to think, the *new* way to be part of the global economy, the *new* way to increase profitability and productivity, the *new* or *best* way to just about do everything. So how can you do it better? How can you manage performance in and for your organisation so that you take it and your people to the next level and achieve your business objectives? How do you attract and retain the people you need to help you do it?

Performance management tools provide a structure and mechanism to evaluate all of your staff – including you – to let everyone know what they're doing well, what they need to change and how everything they do fits into the overall organisational plans.

Tools

Performance management has gained a momentum of its own and is now a huge industry but the tools can be very simple, in fact the simpler the better. Any manager (regardless of level) should know their team members best, what they are good at, what they need to improve. This is not rocket science. Don't

SEX IN THE BOARDROOM

fall into the trap where things become so complicated you start to think you can't do it properly yourself or are tempted to skip through it to save time.

Some of these models are brilliant; others are a total waste of your time and money. Rather than follow someone else's generic model, develop your own performance management program. Your program need not cost a squillion dollars. It simply needs to help you stay focused on what really is important in terms of people management. Over time you will learn what works and what needs adjusting.

KPIs

Not that long ago an organisation discovered keystroke counters. It then became possible to monitor exactly how many times each one of their employees in the booking centre struck their KPI. Management decided to use this as a 'performance target'.

The number of keystrokes per employee was (say) 17,000 keystrokes per day, so that became the KPI and staff who failed to achieve that level would be counselled – not disciplined – to help them improve their performance.

Next time keystroke performance was measured, the average was 18,500 strokes per day.

Management didn't want any below average staff, so the KPI was re-set to 18,500, to encourage all staff to perform above average. The mathematicians among us will spot the fallacy here: they can't all be above average. The employees were set an unachievable target and perhaps an irrelevant one. Had management even stopped to ask whether the number of keystrokes really was one of the things that drove success in the booking centre?

Staff became annoyed and disaffected. Those who could – the best employees – found other jobs. New staff members were hired who had to be trained in the complexities of the role. Line managers were tied up repeatedly counselling staff for not achieving a KPI they knew was faulty, so some of them left too. Customers phoned up and after receiving substandard advice and service from an increasingly inexperienced team, some took their business elsewhere.

Adapting your own model

Some businesses believe performance reviews are probably a good idea but don't do them. Some employees think they are a complete waste of time and don't want to do them because they are suspicious of how the review will be used whilst other businesses and employees love them because they find out how well they're going and what they need to do to fill in the gaps.

If you are already using a performance management program think about how effective it is. Do you consider it a valuable tool? Does it help you to fulfil your role more effectively and to know the people you manage? Is it a document anyone can understand? Is it brief and to the point?

Don't allow yourself to get distracted or confused by the plethora of models available. Have a look at what's around and keep it simple, setting key targets and objectives. Most importantly *set* a date, *do* it and then *review* it to see how it is working. Set, Do, Review. There must be measures you are working towards otherwise you will never know when you have met your targets. Think about the criteria you must meet. Inform your employees about what you're doing, why and what they need to do to fill in the gaps.

Outsourcing

Getting outside help is certainly an option and an excellent one *if* you employ the right organisation to do it and *if* you stay in charge, dictate the terms and style required. However, if you abrogate your responsibility it is unlikely your business or people will benefit. You might just as well throw your money away or better still give it to charity.

Expect to be much wiser after the experience. Make sure the organisation delivers what is genuinely useful to you and then *use* it. This is a huge growth area and organisations are becoming very rich at other's expense, developing review processes which often end up in the bin but worse, waste many of your precious hours before you realise it.

It is important to use the data that you collect to give feedback to your employees and then follow up with them to see how you can assist them to initiate changes and then measure and monitor the progress and results.

Be brave, lead your people, tell them what is working well and build on the other things that need improving. You can do mini reviews all throughout the year and assist your people to think in terms of what's working well and to be constantly reviewing themselves.

Illusion

There's a common illusion about 'arriving'. Somehow, some people think there will come a point where they've made it and they won't have to work at being successful. It will just happen, right? Wrong. To perform, to live any sort of life,

SEX IN THE BOARDROOM

requires hard work and it never stops. You're never going to just 'arrive'.

Scratch the surface of any human being and you will find insecurities, lack of confidence and a whole array of 'issues'. This is human nature. Onlookers think successful people don't have things to contend with; that they're lucky because things come easy for them. Nothing could be further from the truth. Focused, switched-on people are that way because they hold themselves accountable for their thoughts, actions and behaviours and they work hard to change what they don't like.

Manager's review

To perform your role, at some stage you will have to get on with being a manager, make decisions and hold people accountable for their role and for what they said they'd do. Sometimes managers get caught up in being nice and hold back from saying what they need. They subordinate themselves to their employees. There is a world of difference between being a doormat and saying what you need, expecting it to be delivered and treating your team with the respect and dignity they deserve.

SEX IN THE BOARDROOM

Case study

A switched-on, well-respected CEO is convinced that his performance management program helps him to develop his people in a positive way and that it is helping him to achieve best practice. It's done every two years at a huge cost to the business.

One of his new managers was rated very poorly by her employees the first time she completed the review. Significant changes were made to her leadership style over the next two years and her staff said they felt confident with the way she was now leading them. But at her second review, the result showed little or no change. How could this be? Why didn't the test reflect the improvements? She clearly had improved and the results were seen on a daily basis. The secret lies here: the test is conducted anonymously; some of the recipients obviously had a bad day and decided to use it as pay back knowing they would not be identified.

Naturally this manager was very upset about the result – as any of us would be – she'd worked hard to change. She spoke to the team about the results. They were astounded she had received a poor review because they were happy with her performance. She held them accountable for the result and pointed out that they are the only ones who had completed the review so they had to take responsibility for what they were now looking at and discussing. No doubt, they were shocked. It was a good learning experience for them in the short-term and it is hoped they will be honest in the next appraisal of their manager – if she's still there. This outcome is common when people have the opportunity to remain unidentified. They think they can write anything because their identity will not be revealed.

If the organisation's CEO is committed to the process they are likely to believe that the results have delivered an accurate summation of the leader's ability. If the information is true, then so be it. A manager's flaws have been revealed. Be aware that anonymity makes it safe for someone to lie, which can destroy careers without the perpetrator needing to take any responsibility at all for what they've done.

So you think you know them

You've done the reviews. You do them every year and you speak to your team in between when something comes up rather than leaving it to fester. You don't have a commitment to micro management unless it's necessary and then it's only for that period to get the person up to scratch. You're delighted with the way you've held yourself accountable to doing the reviews and you've patted yourself on the back for continuing to follow up and develop each and everyone of your people. Now ponder this: it's one thing to think you've got your team the way you want it but another to actually test it.

Have a look around at your employees and

try to imagine how each one would react to being told - I've noticed that there are a few gaps in your performance this year and we'll need to work on them prior to the review otherwise I won't be able to give you your full performance bonus. What sort of reaction would you get from them? Would they say it to your face or would they whinge behind your back? Would you know what they thought or would they present you with a smile and belittle you afterwards? Think about who would accept the feedback, who would be outraged, if anyone would resign and who in the group would be open to the fact that they need to improve their performance?

Insight

Old thought - I am here to ease the way for everyone to do the job.
New thought - I employ people to help me achieve the organisational goals.

When you come from this Ease The Way perspective you may foster a parent-child style relationship whereby you teach your employees that they can't manage without you, that you need to provide them with everything and that you are ultimately responsible for every decision they make. You find yourself watching what they do, being quick to tell them what they need to do and you probably micro manage them. You may focus on the team's weaknesses rather than finding out their strengths. You assume that you know what is right for the organisation, rather than exploring other options with them. You act as though you'd do a much better job than they would and that's why you provide them with so much useful information. All of the above would generally be with the best of intentions but you know what the way to hell is paved with, don't you?

Summary
When you truly understand how important performance reviews are to the success of the business and to the way your employees perform then you will ensure the reviews get done annually. Set, Do, Review. The hardest bit will be to design them and after that it can be a simple process, costing very little money yet bringing a huge return on investment. Employees can look at them and be clear about what they have to do to achieve agreed outcomes and they can use the document as a basis for regular chats with you.

Being committed to this process helps you to live your performance review each and every day.

You know what works and you do it. You hold yourself accountable for your own agreed outcomes and you talk – kindly but firmly – to your people about what they are doing well and what they need to do to fill in the gaps. You stop bashing your head against a brick wall and instead you walk the talk. Your people know exactly what you want from them and that they can totally trust what you say. They respect you. They won't necessarily like everything about you but hey, who cares. Being in a management role isn't easy and when employees move up to that status they find out just how challenging and difficult the role actually is.

Questions

1. How do you measure your own performance?
2. Do you have annual performance reviews for everyone in the organisation?
3. Do you have mini reviews throughout the year?
4. How do you know that your performance reviews are effective and helping you to improve overall workplace performance?
5. Is the review a long complicated process that costs your organisation thousands (or millions) of dollars and ends up in the bin or filed for later use?
6. Are reviews held somewhere relaxing or could it feel like a murder trial enquiry?
7. Are the results used to acknowledge what your people have done well or to lambaste them for what they haven't achieved?
8. When you've identified areas for change how do you ensure that strategies are implemented so that the person gets support, encouragement and help to change the areas of low performance?

SEX IN THE BOARDROOM

9. Do you develop your managers or just expect them to know how to lead?
10. Do you use these reviews to identify key people who could be brilliant and then develop them for key roles in your business (succession planning)?

Chapter 6
Your Style

Chapter 6 Your Style

There is something magnetic about watching a powerful leader in action. They start impressively and their whole performance indicates that they've done this before and they love it. The people listening to them are glued to their every word. They hardly breathe because they don't want to miss anything. They're smitten and they leave feeling alive, inspired and excited by what they've just been part of and want to do it again. It's an intimate experience.

The speaker has charisma and it radiates in every direction. Groomed to perfection, they have perfected their body language. They know their topic and they deliver it very well using all of their assets. They are the Complete Package.

And then there are other leaders who also have an important message to deliver but – shall we say – their package is not complete. They might be groomed immaculately and they might be nice when you talk to them but they are not dynamic leaders. They're boring. They lack the prowess, magnetism and ability of the polished speaker.

When you're with one of these leaders you know as soon as they utter their first word it is going to be dull, boring and lacklustre. *Are you serious? You want me to listen to what?*

The Incomplete Package may be highly

intelligent but they have not learnt how to get their message across. They think it's all about what they say and they expect everyone else to feel the same way. Big mistake. The spoken word is very important but it is only a very small part of the whole process. There is so much more to it than just opening your mouth and speaking. They might be saying exactly the same thing as the hot leader but it's all in the delivery, the style. They lack charisma and it shows.

Something to remember
People's eyes are glued to the Complete Package and they just can't get enough. How did this happen? Did they wake up one morning, discover they were brilliant at it and that people would line up to see them? No, of course they didn't. They spent years perfecting their delivery and are always looking for ways to improve it. They do their homework and tailor their performance each time. And it works because those in their presence are attentive. Complete Packages exude energy and the audience wants to soak it up. Surely as a leader there would be nothing better than delivering a speech, chairing a meeting or holding a discussion and being treated like this because it means you are having an impact. Your message is getting across and people want to

hear what you've got to say because what you say makes sense.

Not much is remembered about what an Incomplete Package has to say and most people can't wait to escape. For some reason Incomplete Packages can go on indefinitely thinking they're doing a grand job. Perhaps they haven't sought expert assistance or honest feedback about their performance. Perhaps other people are too scared to tell them the truth. If someone has been brave enough to tell them as it is, perhaps they haven't been willing to listen to the advice. Until they do this, they will never become a Complete Package.

All of it

You've perfected the voice, got your style right – now what about your clothes? Are you in the 21st century or are you back in the 70's and recycling clothes for the sake of the environment? I've heard many people (and people who should know better) say that when you purchase classic clothes you can wear them year in, year out. Wear anything that long and it looks old and dated. Keep up to date with your wardrobe – get help with it. Every time people see you, hear you or look at you, remember you are an advertisement for who you are and will be judged quite harshly if you don't look or act the part.

It is worth spending time on this. You don't have to wear expensive clothes but the cut needs to suit your body type. Look in the mirror and be honest with yourself. Have a look in magazines and see what leaders are wearing and how they wear it. Also, check out your colleagues and peers when you're at functions. See whether they have spent time grooming themselves and are good at it or if they just got up and put on the first thing they found. Try not to always be in the corporate black. Look for stylish clothes that give people the message you want them to have about you. I recommend you purchase some new clothes every year so that you continue to add to and upgrade your wardrobe. Suits can last for a couple of years but they also become dated. This of course doesn't apply if you buy the designer labels. It's the whole package and that includes shoes being clean, shined regularly and stylish – not decades old and scruffy.

You'll know when you look hot because people will tell you and then you should just soak it up – it's one of the great pleasures of taking time on your presentation.

Hair

If you want to be a Complete Package, remember that your hair is one of the things people notice first. Have it cut and styled regularly, keeping it modern, clean and tidy. Don't just give it a quick brush in the morning and hope for the best. Hair can make you look brilliant, dowdy, boring or old even if you're not.

For men who are losing their hair, remember that the 'comb-over' look isn't fashionable. If you're losing your hair, then get it cut short. Many men now wear their hair very short and it looks great.

And for women, if you have coloured hair watch for the regrowth. It's not a good look to have a stripe of colour up the centre of your head. Many women look fantastic in their clothes and have obviously spent a lot of time on their grooming, but neglect their hair.

The body

If you want to be firing on all cylinders there are many other things you will need to consider. Think about a racehorse: they have beautiful muscle tone, are regularly exercised, have a good night's sleep and they eat very well. Their whole life is focused on being successful – is yours? And although they

SEX IN THE BOARDROOM

enjoy a good frolic in the paddock with the other horses, they are made to be disciplined because their owners have *plans* for them.

Similarly, many leaders find exercise, quality rest and good food helps them with their whole style. If you want to operate at top level, have a clear head, have a sharp mind and focus on success.

Summary

Become aware of your personal style and know it can make a huge difference to the way people perceive you. Although we're told that we should focus on the 'inside story' rather than what people look like, we know that's not true in the business world. Your presentation can and does make a difference to the opportunities you will be offered and to the success you have. When you look good, you feel good and just like the actors we all admire you can be anything you want to be at any given time – think metamorphosis.

If you are able to nail your look and have a fantastic style, it will make a huge difference to you and the way you operate. Your style should be unique but not at odds with the particular environment in which you are working at any given time. Very few leaders would deliberately develop a style that is going to bore or alienate their audience and those they lead but many are doing just that. Become aware of your particular style and be prepared for someone to tell you the brutal truth.

I have seen people being congratulated for very poor performances and the speaker believes it and goes on to bore future audiences in just the same way. Do not let yourself be so complacent. Even if someone says you were fantastic, be aware that you might have been dead boring. Record yourself, listen to yourself and watch the reaction on people's faces because that will give you an indication of how you're being received. If there's a lot of yawning and people's eyes are wandering around the room then it's time to rethink your delivery.

You can note what works and try different things out each time you're in front of people. Set yourself a challenge. Look at people you admire, emulate some of their characteristics and see how they work for you.

No doubt, like all of us, you will be a work in progress because leadership is one of those things that is always changing. Some of the things that our forebears did are now frowned upon and many of our forebears would think we've gone soft with all this democracy and caring. Each generation brings with it new ideas and new ways of doing things in order to get the same result.

SEX IN THE BOARDROOM

Keep up-to-date with what's happening in this area for your own sake because you don't want to be considered an old fossil. There are many professionals who can help you develop a powerful style and become a Complete Package. It is up to you to be willing to review your style often and to change what needs changing. Actors do it all the time – so can you.

Questions

1. How would you define your leadership style?
2. What's fantastic about it?
3. What have you done to develop it?
4. When was the last time you were in the presence of a leader who had a huge impact on you – good or bad?
5. Name four leaders who have made a huge difference to your leadership style?
6. Does your style get your people to do what you want them to do?
7. Do you upgrade your knowledge about leadership styles?
8. Do you consider that you've made it as a leader?
9. Are you always looking for ways to improve your style?
10. What could you do today to change one thing that you're not happy with that would make a huge difference to your style?

Chapter 7
Workplace Culture

Chapter 7 Workplace Culture

Your workplace culture should provide support and encouragement and be a safe haven for employees. It should also have an acceptable code of behaviour and be progressive in its attitude. When you do it right, it's fantastic to see because the collegiality is obvious. Businesses like this are committed to building the capability and commitment of their people. They provide a work environment where employees can learn and perform to their full potential and each person is committed to the successful achievement of the company's vision, objectives and ongoing sustainability.

It's magnificent to work in an environment like this. Teams are more than superficially pleasant; they genuinely *care* about each other. They want the business to be viable because they want to work there. They want you, their boss to be their boss because they know you're a decent person and although you will hold them accountable for what they do, they know you will also give them leeway when necessary.

These organisations are employers of choice, they win awards, they reap huge benefits from their people and they simply know their people are their best asset.

Two of the most important considerations for a company accomplishing its business goals are the business strategy and the organisational culture that supports it. In many cases the business strategy monopolises attention, while organisational culture is considered a soft issue that can be left to fend for itself. While organisations are thriving, people think it must be easy to have a great culture, that it just happens. Well, I am here to tell you that this couldn't be further from the truth. It's hard work and it's ongoing.

A culture means - *the way we do things around here.* Each business will have their own set of beliefs and expectations and in a workplace these are all brought together. It's a melting pot. It can be fantastic or it can be a hellhole. As the leader, you must be aware of your organisation's culture, know how well it's functioning, recognise what needs to be done to improve it and be committed to ongoing development.

Clear expectations

Ensure your people know you are serious about creating the best environment for everyone to work in – not just the chosen few. When they do something that does not support the culture of your organisation, tell them so. Tell them in a pleasant, non-confrontational way but *tell* them so they can grow and change. Tell your people what you need from them, what behaviours are acceptable, the targets that your business must meet in order to move forward and to be sustainable. There's no need to preach but a gentle reminder won't go astray.

Include values and expectations in your induction program and performance reviews. Focus on the positive behaviours the employee has displayed and then talk about what they can do to improve the workplace culture.

Provide basic details even though they may seem trivial or irrelevant to you so that your staff feel included and part of the process. Many different methods make it easy to communicate – use them to disseminate general information without burdening your people with your problems. Many issues can be addressed more quickly and efficiently as they occur rather than waiting until they have become significant problems down the track. Leaving issues to fester can cause resentment and bitterness.

Size doesn't matter

Since working in the consulting industry, I have seen cultures in many industries and in a number of countries. I've found switched-on leaders in unlikely industries and in unlikely organisations and in all levels of government and sizes of business.

Being an *outsider* means I have seen them

from a different perspective. I was surprised to see that the geographical location didn't have a huge impact on them and neither did the industry. People are people wherever I've worked. They are all trying to earn a decent wage so that they can pay the bills, have a good life and look after those who are important to them.

Management's attitude *to the way they do things around here* impacts the culture as does the attitude of staff. I have seen just how very fragile and how vulnerable cultures are to any sort of change. The whole dynamics seem to reverberate even when one person in the group changes or if there is change in the workplace, friction with management, employees, sickness or problems at home.

The workplaces most successful are where senior management get in amongst them. They don't have an *I'm better than those plebs* attitude. They want to know what's happening in their whole business and they make sure they find out. It takes a lot out of them to do this because they already have enough on their plate but they want to do it because they like their people, they employed them and these are the people that help them to achieve the organisation's ongoing success.

The benefits are huge because the employees know their bosses and they tell them what's really going on in their world. This enables the hierarchy to make sensible decisions that make a difference in the whole business.

I've seen micro, small, large and global corporations operate like this. Size doesn't matter. It's the attitude and commitment that prevails. I've also seen the impact on productivity and profits. I've seen employees take a temporary cut in wages when the business is going through a tough time so that it can survive – that warms anyone's heart because people still have to pay their bills. But when they know the systems and processes are in place and the business is just going through a bad patch, then they are willing to do all sorts of things that aren't considered normal behaviour and where they'd certainly be told by many - *Are you serious, are you nuts - you're doing what, for whom?*

Case study

Imagine the humiliation of being in a key role in an organisation for many years, then along comes a new CEO who takes over and suddenly you have to apply for your own job.

Just recently someone I know faced exactly that situation: Wendy was advised that her role no longer existed and that she could either take a redundancy or apply for the new position. She could have given up and walked away, but she felt a responsibility for the people she was leading and knew that it would create turmoil for many of them if she left. Wendy enjoyed what she did and was proud of her accomplishments. Instead of throwing in the towel, she decided to apply for *her* job.

Six weeks later an interview took place and then three long weeks after the interview, Wendy was informed that she was the successful candidate and invited to take the job.

Wendy initially didn't realise that the new CEO had inadvertently clashed cultures, that they were following their own preferred management model and thought the behaviour was perfectly acceptable. In reality though, the new model wasn't valued, understood or respected in the organisation. The new CEO forgot to imagine for themselves how they'd feel if their own new boss started making big changes without first understanding the organisation and the people in it.

When a new CEO takes the helm they should do their research to find out what has been happening, how the business works and clarify what the existing staff will or will not understand and what will undermine their confidence or security.

As a new leader you can mess things up very quickly. Nothing is more important to getting people on your side than treating them with respect because if you do something that implies disrespect, they will never forget it. We humans are like elephants – we have long memories.

Confirm that there will certainly be changes and help them to understand why the changes will be beneficial and that no changes are being made just for the sake of it. The perception of change for its own sake generally impacts productivity, profitability, morale, absenteeism and turnover in all the wrong ways.

Let your new people know they will be kept informed and that they will be told the absolute truth, not spin. Don't forget to make it clear that they will be treated with respect and compassion during the transition process – without that explicit reassurance you can expect a whole lot of extra resistance.

Watching

It is up to you to inspire, to lead by example so that your employees want to be part of a vibrant business. It is not your role to rescue or treat them like children. They must understand that to pay wages, the business needs to be profitable and they are fundamentally important to creating that profitable business. Without their own hard work and focus, there will be no business and no job.

'Busyness' can divert leaders from taking time out to listen, observe and to recognise what is really happening in their organisation. But management is about people and without them you don't have a business. By not knowing who you have employed, you can inadvertently create a them-vs-us attitude because employees will see a real division between management and employees and won't feel part of the process.

Take time out to observe what's really going on. Have key contacts that can be trusted to give you honest observations of their own as well. Don't surround yourself with 'yes people' because sycophantic personalities only tell you what you want to hear, which is pointless and of no real value when you need to make important decisions.

Managing change

Your organisation's culture is not like the weather that you are powerless to change. You can change what you don't like. You've seen what one square peg can do to the culture. There is no reason why you can't make just as great an impact upon the culture, but in a positive way. If the executives in your organisation think that cultural issues are soft issues and best left alone you may like to give them some hard data that shows the significant impact it has on business costs, productivity and profitability. It can be measured in quantitative terms and this can then be turned into dollar figures.

Strategies and policies should reinforce a notion of 'reward' in a broader context than simply financial reward. The Western world is facing an increasing skills shortage thus giving employees a much broader range of jobs from which to choose. In this context, well-designed, satisfying work, career development opportunities and other intrinsic rewards are seen as being crucial to attracting and retaining key talent. Being committed to developing and maintaining a positive culture can help you become an *employer of choice*, so if you are doing it, make sure you let the world know.

Summary

Understanding the culture in your area of work is the first stage of awareness. If you don't know what it is really like – the good, the bad and the ugly – then it will be difficult to manage and changing it will certainly not be on the radar. Take time out to think about what your workplace culture is like. You can't change what you don't understand and you can't fix problems that you don't know exist.

Most people prefer to work in an organisation that is respectful and rewarding and when I work with leaders in these organisations, it's fantastic to see the way they operate. When I go to work with organisations that allow their workplace culture to be neglected, it can feel like I am entering a hostile environment. Workplace cultures are fragile. Even if your culture is brilliant, you must never assume that it will *stay* that way without intervention and ongoing commitment. Take your eye off the ball for a while and it could take you a long time to get back to where you were. Developing a culture that supports and encourages all who work in your organisation is hard work but worth the investment.

Questions

1. How would you describe the culture of your organisation?
2. Do you know the impact that it is having on the business profitability? How does it affect costs? How does it affect revenues in?
3. Have you ever put a monetary value on it?
4. Does it support you to achieve business objectives?
5. How do you measure your organisational culture?
6. How do you think you could improve it?
7. What are you willing to do to improve it?
8. Is gossip something that is acceptable and commonplace?
9. Is there a safe environment where employees are allowed to say what is important to them?
10. How will you know when you've improved your organisation's culture?

Chapter 8
Thinking

SEX IN THE BOARDROOM

Chapter 8 Thinking

In the modern workplace, someone who is sitting and thinking is typically assumed to be bludging, wasting time and generally being unproductive. If they really were committed to their work, they'd surely be doing something. Goodness knows, there's always something to do.

As a society in general and in the workplace more specifically, we have ceased valuing thinking time, instead seeing it as a virtue to always be busy. Time is limited and there's much to do. No time to waste on thinking just yet. Once on a treadmill it is hard to get off and just about impossible to stand still long enough to see what you really need to see.

It is easy for executives who are stuck on a treadmill to fall into the trap of believing that working longer is the only way to achieve their organisation's goals. But if they don't stop to reflect on their priorities first, working harder and harder is unlikely to change anything for the best.

Luxury of thinking

Thinking is not a luxury. Every single thing you do has a thought behind it. Every decision has a thought behind it. The brain condenses information then emits answers and responses for the owner to ponder. Thinking is *everything*.

Thinking is a great pleasure and you need to

practice it, often. Think of your brain as a coffee machine: put thoughts in at the top where the coffee goes, give it time to percolate and then, out pour new ways of doing things, new approaches, changed ways of thinking for you, your organisation and those you lead. Never, ever underestimate your mind and never, ever under utilise it. It's a gift to be used voraciously. Tap into the deep recesses within and learn how to harness its capacity.

Don't be put off by what other people say when you tell them how much you love thinking and how wonderful the brain is. Their comments may not be complimentary. *They want you to be just like them,* with mind left to go to seed because of being too lazy to explore what the brain can actually do.

Anyone who spends time thinking is an interesting person. When they educate themselves in many ways they become more than just *interesting* – they are incredible, inspiring and a delight to spend time with. You just wonder where all of this information keeps coming from and where they store it and of course then you remember – encased in that head of theirs in a little grey vault.

What was that you said?

I once heard a scientist on a prime time television program talking about entrepreneurs. When he said they were *social misfits* I wondered what planet he was from. I couldn't believe my ears. What concerned me most about this ridiculous comment is that it was not said in jest – he really meant it.

Entrepreneurs are the thinkers in our society, the dreamers. Sometimes they're the kids who don't do so well at school, who would have been sitting in the corridor because of poor behaviour in the classroom. It's common to listen to a powerful leader's story and to hear they never finished school. So remember this next time you are feeling tested by a difficult child: they might not be easy to handle but they might well be one of our future leaders.

Case study

One female student in Year 6 had driven her teachers to distraction for years. Teachers at her school dreaded having her in their classroom. Nobody could work her out. She just sat there and stared into space. I discovered this little gem by pure coincidence and knew immediately I had struck gold. It didn't take long to discover that she was highly intelligent and that I could work with her in the same way as I did with a senior executive. Her powers of reason were incredible. She didn't see the point of doing schoolwork because it was too easy. She was bored stiff and didn't want to waste her time doing this baby stuff when she had far more important things to do and to think about. She had a dirty nose, untidy hair, messy clothes and dirty glasses. She seemed to fit the profile of one of these misfits: unpopular, needy and desperate for friends and the kids she wanted to hang around with would run a mile when they saw her coming.

I found the child a mentor – a successful man in the business world. Together they became quite a team. He taught her key project management skills and together they worked on some projects. Her mentor told her that she had to do well at school and *why*. He told her she needed to keep her clothes clean, hair tidy, glasses clean and *why*. And so she did. She listened to her mentor and within 12 months she was a very different child. She was now a leader in the school, speaking at school assemblies, confidently leading school projects and participating in class. She had friends because she had replaced her neediness with self-belief and the other kids now wanted to hang around with her. The mentor taught her how to develop systems that work in a classroom – she did it and it worked. He felt privileged to be able to contribute and quite surprised to see the difference he made in this timeframe. The child's parents were so grateful to her mentor for taking the time to help their child who had struggled for so many years. The teachers were also grateful because they now had a child who wanted to participate in class and who actively contributed to the dynamics of it.

I'm *fine*, everything's *fine*

The manager is having a workshop to address issues raised by his people. The dialogue starts and surprise, surprise everyone sitting around the table says there's no problem. Participants talk about what's working well, what they're achieving. Then when it touches on what's not working well: *no, everything is fine; no, nothing needs to change.* But this just isn't true. Something does need to change. *We need to talk.*

Scratch the surface and suddenly you will see there are many issues and examples of what is not working well. Managers regularly report they face this situation. The more seasoned leaders know what to do but newer leaders find it very easy to believe everyone is being honest and just get on with it. What they don't realise is that once the door is closed after the meeting, the groups form and *that* is when they talk about the issues.

You need to learn to consider what they're saying. Don't just listen to the words that are coming out of their mouth. Learn to ask key questions and help them to articulate themselves. And if one of your people says it's all fantastic, that is your cue to do a bit of mining and find out what is really going on. Of course there are times when things really are working well and then you can help your people to think about why that is. Why is it working? What did they do to create this situation? And then help them to acknowledge and celebrate it.

What's this then?
I'd like a dollar for every time I've seen *that* look. Their thoughts are written all over their face: *Are you serious?* It seems like an oxymoron to them because their head is spinning and they can't fit everything in to the day as it is, let alone put aside time to do nothing but think.

When people feel like this, the best strategy is to have the sessions away from their office so that they physically have to remove themselves from their chair and come to meet me. We work together in a setting where we are relaxed, we can talk about what they want to achieve and we have a laugh as well. This arrangement allows them to think on the way to meet me and formulate a plan for our time together. They notice that yes, they do feel that their head is spinning and there's never enough hours in the day. I encourage them to evaluate if this is working for them or whether there might be a better way for them to operate yet still achieve their business objectives.

What many of them eventually realise is that they are actually doing a really good job. There are many examples of leaders who expected that working with me would just reveal their inadequacies, not their strengths. The free time allows them to re-evaluate what they're doing well and the gaps they have so they can think clearly and then move out of that stage into action. It stops people from getting caught up in the *whatever I do isn't enough* dilemma where they allow 'busyness' to dominate and keep working 24x7.

The converse is also true. After some time spent thinking, some managers realise that they're not achieving as much as they thought they were. They see that their stress levels are high because they have been doing so many things and not devoting enough time to any one thing in particular. They realise – little by little – that their commitment to excellence has unintentionally begun to slide as they continue to try and fit more into their day.

SEX IN THE BOARDROOM

Case study

Mary was transferred to another department in another country. She had been with the organisation for a long time but this was a totally new environment to her. Everyone in the department was committed to their job and they loved the place. It had a great culture and they dealt with things as they came up. They also had a lot of fun.

Mary's problem? Her predecessor didn't have time to record what her job entailed, so there were no systems or processes in place. Mary was thrown in at the deep end and she had no option but to sink or swim.

There was an important training session coming up for the organisation and she was 'it'. She didn't have time to stop and think about what she had to do, she just had to do it to get it ready on time. This proved successful in many ways because she certainly got the job done but the pressure on her was enormous. There were many tasks that could easily have been delegated but because she didn't have time to think about it, she just had to do it. Mary soon realised that this method was not sustainable and that if she left the role she'd be handing it over to someone who would have to struggle just the same as she had. That isn't Mary's style. She likes everything to be in order.

Mary stopped, took some time out each day and thought about what she had to do to get an effective plan in operation so that the whole team could work effectively and efficiently. There were probably some quizzical looks going on by people initially but in the long-term everyone benefited. Mary spent more time fine-tuning the processes and once this laborious job was done, she actually had a lot more time to work on other specific jobs. Mary was proud and pleased that she had saved her successor from having to go through this stressful period. She was also amazed when she thought back on the amount of time she had wasted when she didn't stop to think.

Summary

The trouble with not thinking is that people can mistakenly believe they're on-track when really they are *on-treadmill.* Remember the Red Queen in Alice in Wonderland? She ran frantically to stay in the same place, knowing that to get ahead she was going to have to run a lot faster. Many business leaders are on a metaphorical treadmill causing them to do much the same. We know that burnout is common with business leaders and they need to stop, get off the treadmill, step back, stand still and think.

Thinking will keep you sane and will help you realise that you don't need to obsess about the business for 24 hours a day. You can't do everything by yourself so treat yourself with the same respect you show your team. You can be more powerful to those you work with when you think and then think some more. You are better able to guide, encourage and help those you lead to see the big picture.

Chapter 9
Continuous Improvement

Chapter 9 Continuous Improvement

Business leaders know that continuous improvement needs to be the norm, not the exception. Regulatory pressures, increasing customer demands and global competition are just a few of the forces behind this need.

The greatest value and return on investment from any change being implemented occurs when the improvement is aligned with the strategic and operational plans for the business. The focus is on how the business can function as one whole unit, rather than on the workings of one department in isolation. Managers are now moving out of their traditional roles to work closely with their teams, increase productivity and make their business more viable. Each employee is an integral part of the business and their work makes a difference to its long-term viability.

High performance culture

Leaders often talk about a high performance culture. But, what does it mean? It means that anyone who has anything to do with the organisation is on the same page: management, employees and all stakeholders. All are committed to achieving organisational goals and any promise made to do something is kept. Luck has nothing to do with peak performers and leaders in industry. They are there because of their streamlined approach to success. It is always the result of hard work. Each contender is focused on the outcomes they need and they constantly review systems and processes to see how effective they really are. They don't lead with their head in the sand. They do their research, are aware of what is happening in their area and are prepared to make the necessary changes. They know they can't do everything by themselves and they don't try. These organisations are innovative and seeking better ways to do things.

Some leaders find continuous improvement easier than others do. If you find it easy then teach others how to do it. If it's hard for you, then learn how to do it. It will take time before you are accomplished in this area, so stick with it until you can see the fruits of your work. Be committed and identify the impact working like this has on your business.

Situational awareness

Pilots are taught situational awareness. They are trained to be aware of what is going on around them at all times. They know what threats exist and where the opportunities lie. They constantly review, keeping their eye on the ball, remembering their objectives and the outcomes that they need to achieve each time they are in the cockpit of their aircraft. The parallels for business are clear. Don't allow yourself to sit back and get comfortable. Pay attention at all times.

Lead by example
I have used a lead by example technique for most of my professional life. I have turned many grumpy unproductive groups into happy teams and even happy competitive teams at other times.

I used my power – ability to influence – to change the landscape of my workplace. I am not saying I consistently won people over but even if they initially despised my direction, work ethic or attitude, they still responded to me and ultimately did change for the better. Some took the path of least resistance and identified with me. Some rebelled and became competitive.

Take heed. This style should only be used when necessary so don't make changes just for the sake of it. I am a firm believer in the old saying if *it ain't broke, don't fix it.* I'm not saying pretend or assume that nothing's broke as your excuse for inaction. However, if it is broke, have a measure of faith in yourself and others that you can and will be able to effect change. Maureen

SEX IN THE BOARDROOM

Case study

Simone is the perfect employee, an absolute pleasure to be around. Intelligent and hard working, she does far more than she needs to do. Simone always thinks about how she can improve what she is doing and has a commitment to producing quality work. The organisation that employs her is regularly downsized and 'rearranged'. She is unhappy with the way the managers keep talking about continuous improvement because the rhetoric doesn't match their behaviour and outcomes. Simone applied for another role in the same organisation but in a different department hoping that the leaders in this area would be up to the job. However, within a few months of starting the new role, it was clear to her that one nightmare position had been exchanged for another and unnecessary change was happening again – more was being expected of the staff, morale was low and many were feeling overworked. It seemed to her that these managers didn't know what they were doing either. Staff had been informed yet again that they had to make budgetary cuts and so they just slashed and burned to get the figures right. Some employees were transferred. Managers were also moved from one department to another without being trained to do their role and being under pressure to continually improve processes they had to make things up as they went along. It did not create the high performance culture they were after. If you are striving to implement positive procedures to create a high performing operation you need to know how the policies impact on the people who are expected to put them in place and to know that your desires and expected outcomes are matched.

Case study

Lewis thought he was a great leader. He was an extrovert, a team player who genuinely cared about those he was managing. He loved the role and had worked hard to develop his own unique style. However, he had a serious problem. He had received two poor peer reviews and his line manager told him that unless the situation was resolved very quickly he was at risk of losing his job. He had not received his performance bonus since starting with this organisation and he was annoyed about that because he had worked hard to achieve his KPIs.

He had transferred from another state to take up the role and had come from a very different industry where his style was valued and worked well. He was now in a conservative business where his style wasn't valued and wasn't working very well at all.

The other team he managed had the mindset of consultants. Meetings were held, plans were formulated and then everyone went and did what they needed to do, with outstanding results. His new team just wasn't like that. They required micro managing because that's what they were used to having and the style suited them.

Whatever Lewis did seemed to be unsuccessful and he had had enough. He was ready to give up but he didn't want to because he'd worked too hard and transferred to another state for this job. The thought of having to look for new work at this moment did not inspire him at all. He made the decision to look at his leadership style and to become aware about what he could do to change it to suit his current circumstances. Lewis wanted to hear the truth from me and of course, I obliged. I encouraged him to look at what he was doing to create the problems in the first place. I also encouraged him to think about the whole situation and then break it down into manageable bits so that he could work on it incrementally rather than feeling overwhelmed. Trying to change everything at once just makes it worse. It causes confusion in the manager and team because whilst they mightn't like the current style – they're used to it and it's normal.

He realised that *he* was the issue that needed fixing and he put in the hard work to do so. He learnt that he needed to stop his happy chappy approach and stop doing everything for his team when they were quite capable of doing it for themselves given they'd all been there a lot longer than he had. He had to stop his rambling, repetitive ways and instead be clear, specific and to the point about what he wanted to achieve with his team. He saw that there was a different way to manage

Chapter 9 Continuous Improvement

his staff and gain the respect of his managers and CEO and we developed an action plan to achieve those outcomes.

Lewis had felt horrible, as if he was losing the plot and didn't have a clue how to handle his seemingly wayward staff. His stress levels were high, he was not eating properly and walking his dogs was a thing of the past. He was working very long hours trying to get everything done.

When this manager changed, he noticed many things and was delighted to see how his staff responded when he was clear with them, when he felt in control and when he was actually doing what he was being paid to do. His team started delivering the right outcomes and he once again felt confident with his managers. Staff and managers began to comment on the difference in his manner. For Lewis, this marked the end of two years in the wilderness and a challenging period.

I was invited to the boardroom when Lewis spoke to his CEO, Human Resources Manager and 2IC about the tremendous changes that he had made to his management style and the impact that these changes had on his people, the productivity, profitability and the whole department in general. He also wanted me to hear that he was for the first time getting his performance bonus.

Seeing a leader take responsibility for what isn't working and then changing those behaviours is very rewarding for any professional because it has an impact on so many people and certainly a huge impact on the overall strength of the organisation.

Summary

If your business isn't operating as effectively as you would like or need it to be then no doubt you are spending many hours thinking about ways to improve your systems and processes and getting into action to ensure your new plans are successful. If your business is operating effectively then no doubt you are spending many hours thinking about ways to improve your systems and processes and getting into action to ensure your new plans are successful. There will always be ways to improve what you are doing and it can be fun to think about them. It can allow you to be creative and to think about possibilities like you did as a kid when you spent hours just imagining what could be. You can think outside the square and encourage your staff to do the same. Keep a record of what you are doing to continually improve your workplace to help you have those thoughts always in your mind. As you become aware of other things you can do, make those thoughts part of your next meeting and assess what benefits they will bring to the business, what the obstacles would be and whether they would be worth implementing. Not every idea will end up being implemented or viable but it will help more people become 'thinkers in residence' and to have continuous improvement embedded in your culture.

Chapter 10
Keep it Simple

Chapter 10 Keep it Simple

What prevents you from keeping your life at work simple? What stops you from coming in to the office each day and achieving necessary tasks? The corporate world has become so complicated that simple isn't even part of the lexicon. For many it has become unmanageable. No wonder so many leaders are tormented by performance anxiety. Whenever someone asks you how you are, the good corporate person will respond by saying 'busy'. They are so busy that they don't have time to identify those things that are most important and genuinely improve their outcomes.

In the corporate world, simplicity has been lost to unmanageable complication. Before leaders wind back and seek to simplify, they've usually been to hell and back. The smart leaders learn from these experiences and rather than continue to be victim to them, analyse why they were so hard and how to turn them around to their advantage. For example, what should you do if you need regular reports from your people and they keep handing over 10 page documents with the 'clue' to what you need to know hidden on page eight? Reading all of that information is a waste of your time, so get them to write all the key information on one page. Think of the time this one change frees up for you immediately and multiply that by how many other reports are coming your way.

It is good discipline for your people to learn to be succinct. If they get used to getting the main points down in less time and learn to come to the point more quickly the benefits will be felt in many situations: in the boardroom, in conversation with their peers, anywhere.

Another example is when your people have problems you know they could work out by themselves yet they keep coming to you, expecting you to solve the problems for them. Create a *No Problem-Only* policy and be willing to listen to their problem only if they have also thought about a way they can solve the issue. This frees up your time and helps your people to stop being so dependent on you.

Open door policy

This would have to be one of the most dubious policies ever created. People walk in whenever it suits them, even if what they have to discuss is not important or urgent and sometimes it is simply an effort to avoid getting started on something they need to do. Despite being the 'boss' you have no control over these constant interruptions. You might need to concentrate on something very important but if you close the door you're seen as breaking policy, being grumpy or not being a real part of the team. It would be hard to measure the loss of productivity caused by this policy and it inadvertently encourages negative behaviour, because the nicer you are as a boss the more free your people will feel to interrupt you. So liberate yourself, change the policy, close the door when you need to and let your people know when you are available to meet with them.

Simple?
As an executive, I don't think your job is ever simple. I think many of us spend much of our time doing the wrong things. Sitting in meetings where no decisions get made. Defending our turf or responding to someone else who feels we have invaded theirs. Managing egos, our own, our boss' and our employees'. Worrying about covering our backside rather than making the right decision. Clarifying expectations or making decisions that staff are perfectly capable of making but won't because of the culture.

Since I have a short attention span and self-destructive tendencies I spend my time as an executive performing alternative tasks instead – making sure my staff have clear expectations, good boundaries and the tools they need to do their job. I spend time with employees at every level finding out what is getting in the way of delivering top value to our customers and fixing it.

And I spend time focusing on key relationships with our partners and being the chief maniac who thinks up programs, products and initiatives that nobody thought was possible and implementing them. Pushing people harder than they thought they could perform and making sure they knew I had their back covered. Developing the next generation of leaders who will be smarter, better and more creative than I am and protecting them from the egos and insecurities of other executives. I also say to people, if your day and your job is so simple and everything is all fine then I wouldn't need someone with your skill set and your compensation to do it.

I think as a business society we get so caught up in tasks we forget to focus on our job. I work with CEOs all the time whose executive teams spend most of their time in their office writing emails to each other or in meetings with each other. Those are *tasks* and they're not even *good* tasks.

I remember being brought in as a change agent for an organisation and having a chat with the CEO who tentatively shared with me that some of the executive team did not 'like' me.

At a subsequent meeting I asked, "How are the numbers?"

They responded, "Great, up significantly."

I said, "How is employee engagement/morale?"

They said, "Oh, seems to be very positive, people are excited."

I said, "How is customer feedback?"

They said, "They really seem to like the new initiatives, products and so on."

I said, "What was it you wanted to talk about again?"

They said, "Never mind."

I relate that somewhat tongue in cheek, but how much time do we spend on piddly issues? Mark

Case study

Most of the issues that have affected my performance in managerial positions and made it difficult to keep it simple were related in one way or another with corporate policies, management styles, business processes and personality traits that are a mirror of the corporate culture.

Many of the decisions I have made as a manager required the involvement, commitment and participation of professionals belonging to different functional areas in the organisation.

When organisations operate with a clear emphasis on the operational processes inherent to individual departments then a siloed vision of business prevails. When senior management dismiss the impact of this mindset over an organisation where cross-functional processes would better achieve business agility, managing projects with different functional departments involved becomes a recurring nightmare.

In companies with a conservative culture, I have found the focus on the detail of each manager's own operations to be an enormous obstacle to the strategic thinking required for the making of decisions with real business impact.

When I have managed projects with transformational impact, senior management usually dismissed the need to invest in complementary facilitation of the change process because they didn't understand the relevance and importance. This adversely affected my efficiency in executing these high impact projects because I had no mandate or resources to manage the behavioural variables associated with the organisation, its culture and its business processes.

In projects where a rapid, professional response was necessary to provide true customer satisfaction, bureaucratic processes and observance to rigid administrative policies have prevented me providing a proper professional solution.

On occasion I felt frustrated when my former boss – an insecure practitioner of micro management – obsessively denied each one of my attempts to introduce a system of incentives to reward, compensate and recognise the extraordinary performers in my department. He justified this by invoking blind observance to rigid corporate cultures. Octavio

Insight

I think the biggest issue is the spiralling impact of not knowing how to delegate. There are many type-A personalities in executive roles who do not know how to break the bonds of their mentality: *if it is going to be done right, it has to be done by me.* So what do they do? They do all the things that have to be done but could have been done by someone else instead of focusing on the things that really need to be done just by them.

So what is the answer? Learn to delegate. If you handle everything that comes across your desk directly, there isn't enough time for you to do the things that are a part of your organisational goals. Bob S

Decision making process

When working with anyone in a management role I notice many are not achieving what they want to achieve. They race from one thing to another. When these same managers have a professional support person in their life things change. They take a deep breath and are so glad that they finally got some support for themselves. They see what they need to do to be effective in their role. They understand what they need to do on a daily basis to become a respected leader. They start to value personal boundaries, because they know that without them, life is chaotic and an endless stream of unfinished work. Having their personal weekly meeting can make the difference between years of head banging experiences and getting ahead, learning what needs to be done, doing it, identifying what needs tweaking and then tweaking it.

Success

Success is not what I thought it was. Success is not *only* having a conflict to resolve or finding solutions to help customers or coming up with some big project to save the business money. Success includes day to day matters like communicating a team move in a positive way so the person can see the positives of the move, thereby maintaining morale and making it easier for the next team leader.

Success also means the small changes one makes because of self-improvement. So success is smiling more and being more relaxed because you do the other tasks well now.

Success is being respectful to other people but

not being walked over. So success is being brave enough to have the difficult conversations with these people. Success is becoming more self-aware. This self-awareness leads to personal development and an increase in confidence and control. Domenic

Case study

We've conditioned ourselves to believe that we must be interrupt-driven in modern society. If a phone rings, we jump to answer it. If someone comes to the door we open it up and let people in. This is because we think that working as a team is so important and we don't want to give the appearance that we aren't team players.

In the corporate world, some companies have even gone so far as to remove cubicle dividers and push all the desks close to each other.

There may be some workers for whom such closeness breeds teamwork, but for people in a role that requires them to create solutions or solve problems that require some thinking, it is much better if they can have the freedom to close their office door.

In corporate culture, I believe that such people work better if they are not interrupted by people 'stopping by' their office or their workspace. I think it is much better to use email when possible to initiate meetings because it is something that can be read when the recipient determines they are in the right mind frame to read it.

SEX IN THE BOARDROOM

> In short, manners and respect for the workspace of others can go a long way towards creating a workplace of people who are following purpose and plan, rather than being interrupted by people who need everything yesterday. Bob

Summary

It's a paradox. Keeping it simple seems so very difficult. The things that keep us from achieving what we want to achieve are so complicated and so numerous that people don't even know how to articulate them. Ask them what has been keeping them so busy and they're likely to say 'Just, well, stuff'. This is very revealing. If they can't actually remember what it is they've been doing, is it really likely to be truly important? Are they doing time or are they doing the things that will make a difference to the business? They need to simplify their stuff-filled schedule and pare it back to the things that matter and the things that make a difference to their outcomes.

Keeping it simple may be one of the hardest things you will ever do but once you have achieved it you can kiss performance anxiety goodbye. You will have your systems and processes in place, you will have your teams functioning at a manageable level, you'll have learnt the art of delegation and you won't keep doing what doesn't work.

Chapter 10 Keep it Simple

Australia once had a prime minister who told the country's citizens that 'life wasn't meant to be easy'. I would love to have had a dollar for every time the media has repeated his words. Rather than saying what he did and accepting that life is going to be tough, he could have shared insights far more illuminating and helpful. It would have been far more beneficial if the media had quoted him explaining the difference it makes to being a leader when the 'keep it simple' principle is embraced.

Imagine having years of gentle reminders to keep things as simple as we can as often as we can.

Questions

1. What stops you from keeping it simple?
2. What stops you from getting caught up in unnecessary drama in the workplace?
3. What stops you from getting caught up in 'problem-thinking'?
4. What empowers you to say what you want with confidence and clarity?
5. What gives you the courage to draw up a 'plan' and stick to it because you know how beneficial it is to you?
6. What assists you to focus on what's important?
7. How do you know what you're doing will get you to where you need to be?
8. How do you know when you're wasting time?
9. What have you tried to do to keep it simple?
10. What are the benefits when you keep it simple?

Chapter 11
Meetings

Meetings are an integral part of the business strategy and an important way for an organisation to keep in touch with what is happening. However, they can be an over-used time wasting exercise with leaders racing mindlessly from one meeting to another without having time to prepare for the meeting or to assess whether they are of benefit. If you calculate the real cost of meetings, you will find the answer scary. Lost productivity, time spent just getting to meetings, not to mention the cost of bringing in people from interstate or overseas. Even in the same building people have to interrupt what they are doing, leave their desks and when they return to their workstation it may take just as much time to get their thoughts back to where they were beforehand. Your meetings are an investment: an investment by the company in achieving the results it demands, an investment by you as a leader in achieving the results you need from your people. It is up to you to ensure you – and your organisation – get the best return on that investment.

Bang for the buck

Have you considered the amount of time you spend in meetings and the real value you get out of them? Every organisation has a budget, an allowance of money and time with which it must achieve its goals. Do a meeting audit. Ask yourself why you are having the meeting, why you are attending it and what you expect to get out of it. Then be willing to talk to your people about meeting procedure, meetings in general and different ways you could achieve the best outcomes. Audit each meeting to check that it is helping the business to progress in the right direction.

An agenda

Everyone sitting around the table has their own agenda and some probably haven't prepared for the meeting. For them it is just something else they have to do. Their head is still filled with the work they've just left and they're probably wondering how long this will take. When you chair a meeting it is up to you to be organised, to prepare for it, to keep the meeting on-track and to have high expectations of all participants. Think carefully before each meeting and always plan for them.

Do this in a relaxed place where you can write an agenda. Meetings must have a purpose and need to provide a return on investment in the salary sitting around the table, the lost productivity and the time spent getting to and from the meeting.

Agendas help you to prepare for a meeting. I have found that many people avoid writing an

Chapter 11 Meetings

agenda because they don't know how to do it. Just try it. It might take awhile in the beginning but once you're used to it, it only takes a few minutes.

The agenda is like a road map for the meeting. You know where you're going, where the route will take you and where you're likely to end up. List the main topics of discussion – just a few words for each topic. Keep the number of items to a minimum and mentally allow a certain amount of time for each item to be discussed. If you have set one hour for the meeting, then keep to one hour.

When I lead a meeting like this I feel empowered, switched-on and confident of why I am in the meeting. It's not just another meeting because I've spent time thinking about it and I know the key outcomes to be achieved. Others at the table are happy because someone who knows what they're doing is leading them.

Your investment

Meetings are not just a get-together they are an investment. As a key person in the business you are accountable for seeing that outcomes are delivered to all involved. It's your responsibility to ensure that everyone has their say but to also manage the whole process from beginning to end. You will have people with every type of personality: consensual, sharing, bossy, bored, disinterested, intimidating, impatient, shy. It is important to be aware when someone is dominating the show or when someone isn't participating. If they are at the meeting then there is something they are expected to contribute, otherwise they'd still be at their desk. At regular intervals, summarise key points and move on, always keeping your eye on the clock.

Five minutes before the end of the meeting, let people know you're about to sum up. Identify what you have achieved, note whether you have covered everything, if follow up is required or if you can leave things as they are. Discuss next steps and create an action plan with clear responsibilities and timeframes for each person. Identify when the next meeting will occur, its purpose and timeframe, the format it will take, the way it will be delivered and your expectations. Thank people for their contribution, saying that it's been a productive meeting. Make it clear that you look forward to receiving their action plan with what they have achieved by a specific date so that the next meeting will meet business objectives as well.

This style works well because it's like a mini project. Everyone knows what is expected of them. They know that they have to perform and that the meeting is not an opportunity to have a snooze.

Benefits to you

- You know why you're there: your goal is at the top of the agenda. You can focus on it the whole meeting and keep bringing your attention back to it. It's too easy to get caught up in the 'stuff' of other people around the table, lose sight of what you're meant to be doing and then – oh dear – the meeting has ended and you haven't covered what you should have.
- Time spent in meetings is productive, not wasted and there is less time lost in chitchat.
- Participants know why they are in the meeting and what is expected of them.
- You keep speakers on-track because you manage the whole process.
- You make real dollar savings for your organisation because there are no hours wasted in under-performing meetings.
- By keeping it simple it is easier to maintain interest and momentum.
- Participants know that when you are chairing a meeting, there is clarity and certainty about the meeting and its outcomes that might otherwise be missing.

SEX IN THE BOARDROOM

- The transition back to each participant's desk after the meeting happens more efficiently.
- When you lead effective meetings your confidence increases and you feel more powerful in the role.

Case study

A junior executive felt totally inadequate when she was in a meeting. A naturally shy person, she just sat and listened rather than become involved and tuned out when the meetings were boring. She felt that everyone was older and more senior than she was, they knew much more than she did and that she really didn't have much to contribute. Besides, they wouldn't listen to her anyway so what was the point? She felt like a victim – an ineffective, submissive player amongst very important people who knew far more than she probably ever would. With the assistance of a professional colleague and by taking time out to assess the situation she realised that she did have options. She decided to act and in doing so discovered the secret to being productive in meetings and contributing to them. She now goes into each meeting to see who is there, what their personal agenda is (as opposed to the meeting's agenda) and to observe their style.

This young executive came to realise the importance of planning and developing objectives for each meeting and learnt the value of taking time out regularly to think and reflect. Doing so helped her focus on important issues and to stop getting caught up in everybody else's advice or in her own worries about not being good enough. She realised that she could continue to worry about feeling ineffective or she could do something about it. She decided to discuss the outcomes with her manager and found that by taking the time to identify what she personally got out of each one of them, she gained clarity. It helped her to identify the objectives and outcomes of the meeting rather than going from one meeting to another, wondering if she'd simply wasted her time.

SEX IN THE BOARDROOM

Insight

I really like to limit meetings but one of my business partners always wants more meetings and with her, there is no such thing as a short meeting. I am seriously in avoidance mode because of the way she impacts my 'talking time' versus 'doing time'. She uses meetings to railroad, to ensure that she gets what she wants – she seems to think that allowing someone else the time to speak is the same as listening, but it isn't.

So if someone else speaks, she'll stay quiet for a moment then simply go back to the reasons why she is right, why her way is the best, why everyone else is wrong and it is as though no one else even spoke. This scene is repeated until we finally give in. Then later when her plan isn't successful she has the nerve to claim that it was 'our' decision to do it that way.

I have tried managing this in so many different ways. Now I keep her honest. She has been railroading about a particular project just recently, expecting me to let her have her own way. Instead, I said, "It is clear you are committed to doing this and it isn't actually going to matter what I say. You want to do it, so do it. But OWN it, take responsibility for it and don't try to railroad me so that later on you can argue it was a group decision." This really took her back but seems to have worked. It has taken me over two years to get to this point though. So yes, an agenda is a must but it is important we remember that the purpose of the meeting is not to railroad towards her (or my) desired outcome. It is to end up with the resolution that is right for our company. Louise

Summary

Meetings are one of the traditions that have happened with groups of people since time immemorial and of course they will continue. They are essential. People in the business world need to be able to communicate, to plan for future development, to be clear on what is happening in various parts of the business and to know how well the business is going.

Do most businesses need the number of meetings they normally have? The short answer is no. Do businesses in general do an audit of their style of meetings, delivery, outcomes? The short answer, no. Are they evaluated for effectiveness? Short answer, no. I encourage you to think carefully about how you can get the information you need to ensure ongoing growth and success in your organisation. Think how you can do it in a variety of ways and formats instead of always having the face to face meeting. Be creative. Plan to reduce the meetings you have by at least 30% over a specific period, document the benefits and disadvantages whilst remaining focused on what is essential.

I have met few leaders – very few – who actually plan for a meeting and are clear about a meeting's objectives. And I've met even fewer leaders who sit down after the meeting to identify what worked well, what was achieved, what happened that wasn't expected, what didn't work and what could have been improved.

Questions

1. Do you really need every one of those meetings?
2. Do you have a clear plan for the meeting and keep to it?
3. How much does each meeting cost your business?
4. Are you excited at the end of the meeting because of the number of essential decisions that have been made?
5. Can you see how each of the meetings is making a huge difference to the organisation's productivity and profitability?
6. Do you achieve the outcomes you want?
7. Do you use technology to have a meeting?
8. What other ways could you gain the same information?
9. Do you personally prepare for every meeting that you have or do you just sit around the table and wing it because you've been too busy to prepare?
10. Do you assess each meeting when it's finished for the value it has delivered?

Chapter 12
Stress

SEX IN THE BOARDROOM

Insight

When insights are trying to wriggle out and get into the conscious state they can cause the mind a lot of angst. They can cause worry, anxiety and a state of confusion.

Chapter 12 Stress

Stress can be a killer. It bubbles away in our bodies like a volcano waiting to erupt. Not understanding, underestimating and not monitoring your stress levels over a long period of time can lead to burnout, to developing a no-holiday policy, to pushing yourself to achieve more and more without a break and to lose sight of how much stress is impacting on you. It can bring about the demise of the career to which you have given so much of yourself and seriously impact upon the other things that are important to you outside of the workplace.

Most leaders keep such hectic schedules that they don't even realise they're stressed, let alone acknowledge that stress could harm them. They ignore signals of a condition that if left unchecked could take away the ability to be a powerful leader, not to mention other good things in life like having fun, laughter, feeling positive, acknowledging and enjoying what you've achieved. The higher up the ladder you are, the more you are likely to ignore the signals. *It won't happen to me.* The invincibility of our adolescent years is still with us and even though we hear about what it can do to people and see others fall by the wayside we doggedly resist accepting that it could happen to us.

Some leaders feel as though they are being self-indulgent when or if they focus on stress.

Sometimes they wake up before it's too late and change their behaviours. Others aren't so lucky, ignoring the warning signs until they are struck down with a major debilitating illness or worse. Some have an epiphany at that point, changing their behaviour because they realise how fortunate they have been just to survive. For others it is too late.

Stress needs to be managed. Only one person can take charge of stress in your life and that person is *you*. Stress levels can be very hard to recognise in yourself as you continually adapt to new, higher stress levels. Once you recognise and acknowledge how important it is, you can quite easily measure the impact stress has on your business, on yourself and on everyone else in your business.

Case study

I have been trying to spot the early warning signs for years in the hope of teaching myself how to nip stress in the bud, but I rarely succeed. I know I can be difficult to get on with when my stress is out of control. I will generally sabotage myself in some way before I get the wake up call yet again.

Leadership is important to me and I refuse to undermine my years of hard work by being unpleasant, impatient and too demanding. I know from experience that stress sneaks up on me and changes my personality and behaviour without me being aware of it. So now I have strategies in place to recognise and avert the problem before it escalates. It still feels hard for me to take time out from pushing myself to succeed because I have so much I want to accomplish and not enough years to do it in. This is something I have to keep learning and may well do for the rest of my life.

I have found that when I have insights into my behavioural patterns and self-limiting behaviours that they indeed seem weird and back to front. My insight is that the reason I've kept pushing myself is because I was scared that if I didn't I would become lazy and then be happy with doing little and achieving little. Knowing me and the natural drive and energy I have this makes no sense and I am glad that I am now aware of this pattern that was not helping me to be the professional (or person) I want to be.

To avoid a build up of stress and burning-out

I am learning that I need to take time off regularly and to work less hours. I also know that I have to have fun and incorporate other things into my life and not only talk about my business. This is hard for me because I just love what I do because I only work in areas that I feel passionate about. I could work 24x7 quite easily (in my mind) but I know that I can't because I burnout and get sick.

I am delighted to continually discover how easy life can be and how much more pleasant people are to be around when *I'm* not stressed. Previously insurmountable problems transform into small issues that can easily be fixed. Verity

Burnout

Why are more and more leaders burning-out? Why is this happening when we are flooded with information about maintaining balance in our professional and personal lives? Significant research is undertaken on this issue but the findings are not being converted into action within workplaces.

The failure to address stress places a huge burden on almost everyone involved. It is hard to measure the cost to business but it must surely be huge. Many leaders say that when their organisation's key people are stressed-out that it is much more difficult for them to lead effectively or give clear directions to their managers and employees. The reason is because *they* don't stop to reflect on what is working well and what needs tweaking and they are much more likely to make decisions on the run that may benefit in the short-term but are not in the long-term interest of the organisation.

You could be justified expecting that in the 21st century we'd all be so 'switched-on' to the problem that it wouldn't be an issue anymore. Instead there seems to be a global 'stress epidemic' and if the current state of inaction continues it will cost government, business and community significantly. It would not be the least bit surprising to see medical claims for stress-related mental and physical problems and workplace injury increase significantly over the next few years.

Leaders will avoid taking holidays or time-off because they are stuck on a treadmill that is set at '10'. They may feel as though their head is in a vice and whatever they do isn't enough. It will be hard to talk to someone about how they feel when they fear exposing themselves to being seen as a weak link. Besides, they *should* be able to manage what is going on without help, right? Wrong.

The worst-case scenario is the leader who has worked very hard for years, done great things for the business but neglected other areas of their life because they really hadn't had time to do it or to think about it. They ignored what people told them because a stressed leader always knows best and what would *they* know anyway? And then they retire, ready to get into other things they have wanted to do for years. They have no plans in place because they think it will just happen naturally, they'll just love retirement because they've earned it and waited for it for so long. They have a break, they take off around the world or do whatever else they wanted to do, but after a year they're bored stiff and wondering what on earth to do with themselves. Or even worse than this they get ill or a long-term relationship breaks down – one which they *were* going to thoroughly enjoy because now they've got time to put into it, only problem is they find they have nothing in common. And it's not uncommon for people to die shortly after they retire. Wow – now that's something to work hard for, isn't it?

Case study

I know what happens if I don't manage my stress levels. I lose my passion, enthusiasm, whinge a lot (to myself) and find it painful to deal with other people. My patience drops significantly and I try to avoid speaking with people for long on the phone. *Let's just get this over with, shall we?* What really worries me is that I'm *much* more likely to do what other people say instead of standing back and assessing whether it really is the best plan to follow. And once I'm in that mode, it is a downward spiral because I am giving *other* people my power yet *I* am still accountable and *I* will be the one who is held responsible for outcomes and *I* have to bear the consequences. I notice myself thinking that *they* know better than I do so I should listen to them. But the truth is, they have their own agenda and it's in their best interest if I do what they want me to do.

And other things happen if I don't *stop*. I find myself apologising far more than I should. I become much more likely to give people useless advice and mind *their* business because I'm charged and unable to stop. It's embarrassing to realise this later, when I'm not so wound up, but it's hard to stop it when it's happening even though I know I'm doing it. Steven

Summary

Think of a clock that has been over wound one too many times. It doesn't work; it just refuses to go properly. We are very similar. When we keep pushing ourselves, we don't work effectively either. It can take driven people a long time to see this in themselves and to even admit to themselves that they're stressed.

It's not about *if* you are affected by stress, it's *how much* you're affected by stress. The very people who should take stress very seriously tend to underestimate its impact upon them. They fail to understand or monitor their stress levels and over a long period this can have devastating effects upon their careers, health and personal lives.

Practice safe stress. Wait for too long and you might find yourself with a much bigger problem than you bargained on. It is better to prevent your stress escalating than it is to deal with it later when you have a swag of additional health and emotional issues wrapped around it.

You might be one of the lucky ones who doesn't get sick or is able to recover quickly but the odds are that you are *not* one of the lucky ones. So look after yourself, protect yourself. Don't become a statistic. Don't work tirelessly for many years making a huge difference to the business and the people you are responsible for, only to succumb to some catastrophic health problem. Take charge of your health and get a team on your side who help you to stay really well so that you can continue to achieve your potential and live a quality life.

Questions

1. What do you know about stress?
2. Do you think it relates to other people and not to you?
3. What do other people act like when they are very stressed?
4. What do you act like when you are very stressed?
5. Do you have systems in place to recognise when you are stressed?
6. What do you do to manage your stress levels?
7. How do you monitor your stress levels?
8. If managing stress were 5/10, what would your levels be right now?
9. What would you like them to be?
10. Do you have regular check ups to check for your stress levels?

Chapter 13
Ignorance is Bliss

Chapter 13 Ignorance is Bliss

You might be reading this book because the name caught your eye or because of the chapter titles and cartoons but I wrote it because I want you to become *aware*. Aware of what you are doing right now, aware of the fantastic things you are doing as a leader and also to dig deep to find out if you have any *self-limiting* behaviours. When leaders do the *dig* they realise that ignorance isn't bliss. This chapter can help you to become aware as to how often you operate in Blissful Ignorance. Awareness is paramount: it has *purpose*.

Swift mind

Many leaders have a quick mind and they can move from one thing to another easily. Developing concepts and moving to the next level is often very easy for them. They are Think, Do, Done It sort of people and want to achieve as much as they can so they can get onto their next project. If you have a mind like this you'll need to be aware that it can drive some workers a tad crazy because they never know what their manager will come up with next. Many employees just do whatever they are asked and even if the manager asks them if their workload is okay, if they're managing well the employee is likely to say yes, when they mean no. Most people have a fear of rank and are too scared to tell the truth so they keep pushing themselves to do whatever is asked of them. And the manager is unaware they are causing uncertainty and stress in their staff.

Pat on back due

I work with many leaders who are absolute gems. Their organisation and people are incredibly lucky to have them. They work hard, they care about their people and nothing is too much for them. They also achieve business outcomes. The only problem is that they are Blissfully Ignorant of this fact. They are stumped when I ask them about their leadership qualities and although these qualities are very clear to me, it has never crossed their mind before. They do what they do because they love it and they are driven by their ethics and decency. Their goal is to motivate others, instil enthusiasm, empower those they lead and achieve prosperity for their business. These sorts of leaders make themselves approachable, build relationships and earn the trust of their staff. They make sure their employees feel happy, comfortable and motivated because they know they get better outcomes when they follow this approach.

They might never reflect on why they do things this way or why they are this type of leader. They probably don't have time to do this and even if they

Chapter 13 Ignorance is Bliss

did, would consider such reflection self-serving. When I speak to them about the fact that they are really decent leaders they are embarrassed. They think that patting themselves on the back is being egotistical which is not their style and not the reason why they went into management in the first place.

When I'm working with these gems it can take a long time to convince them that they are outstanding at what they do. I encourage them to think of a leader they admire and the qualities that person has and then to think about the similar qualities they might just have. It takes them awhile to realise and to accept that it's okay to acknowledge themselves for what they do rather than beat up on themself over the occasional occurrence that didn't go the way they intended. One mistake and they will hammer themselves for days but their many successes won't be enjoyed for even one second.

It's tragic. It is imperative they learn to think about what they do well. It builds confidence, self-esteem and helps them become even more effective in their role.

It is also tragic when a leader thinks they're doing a grand job when in fact they are Blissfully Ignorant of how ineffective they are.

SEX IN THE BOARDROOM

Case study

A decent, caring senior executive in a large organisation has no idea that she is driving her staff crazy with her constant demands and by changing her mind at the last minute. She asks her personal assistant to develop projects and then at the last minute changes her mind so that her assistant has to do much of the organising all over again. To this day, she doesn't realise that she is negatively affecting her staff and the business outcomes because nobody will tell her. The CEO won't, the executive team wouldn't dare and of course the staff don't feel it's their place to do so. So she continues on her merry way, Blissfully Ignorant while inadvertently wreaking havoc on those around her. But how can she change if no one is willing to tell her? This leader is a decent hard working woman who has given far more than she needed to over many years. Not only would she be surprised if she were made aware of how her behaviour impacts on the whole organisation, she'd be embarrassed and mortified to know that she was the only one unaware of it.

The observer

So, you think that there may be a little truth for you in this chapter and that sometimes you unintentionally lead in Blissful Ignorance. You've even heard yourself thinking it and heard the statement from people you associate with. What does this mean for you as a leader? How can you change your style from Blissful Ignorance to Purposeful Awareness?

Be the observer of your own behaviour. Listen to what you say to those you lead. Ask key people who will tell you the truth and with whom you have developed a trusting relationship whether they think that you lead in Blissful Ignorance. Have a look at the questions at the end of this chapter, think about your answers and see if you uncover some useful insights.

Aha moments

Remember what it was like when you first started driving a car? You knew what you wanted to do; you wanted the freedom that driving a car would give. You might have expected it would be easy but what you probably found is that it was more complicated than you thought it would be. It probably took a long time before you felt confident and competent behind the wheel and it was probably quite some time before experienced drivers respected you.

Just like learning to drive, uncovering the behaviours that have kept you blind to your Blissful Ignorance management style will probably be confronting, challenging and difficult. You'll probably have that squeamish feeling in your stomach as you think about it. However, it is a wonderful moment when you start to have insights about behaviours that are not working for you. It's even better when you get into action, change what you don't like and then start to recognise the benefits that your new behaviours are creating.

Often managers find that such an insight will leave their mind as quickly as it came and that they forget them because they are working on other things. They find that by keeping a record of each insight it enables them to acknowledge the behaviour they wanted to change, to articulate the changes they have achieved and then to consciously praise themselves. They can then feel proud of what they've done and encouraged to continue to change and improve their leadership style. Another unexpected outcome of writing down these insights is that they lead to more insights about their leadership role and style.

Confucius say
Whenever I am trying to integrate a new behaviour, I have to be prepared to work hard until it's entrenched into my behaviour. I seem to go through a period of confusion when the new behaviour is not yet embedded and the old one is still alive and well. The transition phase will depend upon the length of time for which I have been living and working with the old behaviour. I have also found that when I am

stressed or feeling pressured, the old behaviour is much more likely to return until I become aware of what I am doing again and jump into the preferred behaviour again. Being *aware* of what is happening helps me to stay committed to my *purpose*: adopting the new behaviour and not allowing myself to slip back into my old ways. This can be a difficult time so it is important to acknowledge that you are not perfect and that you will make mistakes. Give yourself full marks for having the courage and conviction to continue with this change. And just note that some days you will do it a lot better than others. Charles

Ignorance wasn't bliss
Working some years ago I came across someone just like this. I'm a positive person and always like to get on with everyone but this took me by surprise because I'd never seen it acted out so cleverly and with total ease. The CEO had no idea that in his team was one such person and this person had been a close friend for a long time. What was clear to the other directors and staff was that this person worked tirelessly for the CEO, smiled when he was around, couldn't do enough for him but the moment his back was turned she belittled him. Anyone who listened heard how

poorly he performed, what he did wrong and how ineffective he was as the CEO. Why would you suspect someone like this? The bottom line is: you wouldn't. And as she was lambasting the CEO she had a lovely smile on her face.

It took me a long time to work out what was happening and I found it confusing. How could someone so friendly and supportive be so horrible? The worst thing is that this person thought their behaviour was perfectly normal. She had no idea that it was dysfunctional and that other people did not enjoy the way she spoke about this fantastic CEO. They listened because they couldn't get her out of their office.

These square pegs need to be weeded out so that the rest of the staff can get on with their job. Watching them in action would be funny if it wasn't so serious and they have victims everywhere. It's like an abusive relationship. It's bizarre to most of us but if you come across someone like this in the workplace then you'll have your work cut out for you to first identify and then manage them.

To this day the CEO does not know that one of his team is like this and even though they have both moved on in their roles they are still close, meet regularly for social occasions and he thinks she is one of his best friends. And she still does exactly the same as she's always done – is nasty behind his back and to his face is lovely, kind and acts like the person you would want in your life as a best friend, colleague and support. Genevieve

Don't be a Lionel

Many years ago when I had a young family and was working part time, I reported to a manager called Lionel. He was an absolute horror, an ex-army sergeant who ran the organisation as though it was a boot camp. His face generally looked like it was made of steel, he ordered everyone around as though they were his foot soldiers and expected things to be done right then and there. He was your basic nightmare package and then some.

There was no room for creative thinking with Lionel – we were to do as we were told, no questions asked. It's a wonder he didn't call us to attention then get us to drop to the floor and give him 10.

Lionel thought his management skills were brilliant and as far as he was concerned, no changes were required. Everything was congruent with his belief system: he was paid to keep staff in line and keep customers happy so that they would keep spending their money. Why would he consider changing a thing when it was all working so well?

To this day, I am not sure whether the

management team who kept employing him was happy with him, if they knew what a martinet he could be, or whether they liked having an attack-dog in the place because it saved them from having to do anything. Or perhaps like me they were simply too scared to say anything to him? Eunice

Summary

As the leader, you need to be *aware* and have *purpose*. Be focused, switched-on and have eyes in the back of your head. Know what you're brilliant at and get people around you who are brilliant at what you are not. Surround yourself with people who will be honest, so that it is not possible to slip into Blissful Ignorance. Look deep, see what needs changing and change it.

If you are conscious now that you have adopted a Blissful Ignorance management style, then you need to shake yourself into Purposeful Awareness. Start now.

You might feel embarrassed to uncover habits that have led you to practice this principle. Yes, it is challenging, confronting and takes time – as if you haven't got enough to do already. But ask someone who has successfully uncovered and changed their behaviours: *although laborious at first, they say, it is worth the effort and the payoffs are many.*

Those you lead and others you associate with will see you as authentic, a person who leads with integrity and can be trusted. They will value your awareness and admire your purpose. They will trust your insight and respect that you are willing to change what isn't working, when others would find it too challenging and confronting to bother with. In the long run, being aware of how you lead, being willing to change what doesn't work and regularly monitoring yourself makes you a more powerful leader and creates a much better workplace than leading from Blissful Ignorance.

Questions

1. What does the statement Ignorance is Bliss mean to you?
2. What does the statement Purposeful Awareness mean to you?
3. When do you lead from these perspectives?
4. What is the impact on those you lead this way?
5. How productive is it for all concerned?
6. Do you think long and hard about the organisation as a whole and whether Blissful Ignorance is inadvertently supported by the culture?
7. Do you ask people you trust (only a few) for their honest, gentle feedback?
8. Do you work with an executive coach to uncover the behaviours that need to change?
9. Do you measure everything you do for the business both qualitatively and quantitatively?
10. Do you acknowledge yourself for having the courage to be aware of your roadblocks?

Chapter 14
Fear

SEX IN THE BOARDROOM

Insight

When I challenge my fears, take time out to identify what they are and what I need to do about them, I feel liberated and go from strength to strength. A wonderful feeling. It is something I need to do regularly. Because I like to be involved in a number of projects at the same time, I can end up with thoughts racing around in my head and feeling as though I am not making headway. Taking time out to think about what I'm really doing and addressing my fears allows me to remain enthusiastic and passionate about what I am involved in. It allows me to focus on my long-term goals. I encourage you to do the same because the pay-offs are huge and well worth the effort.

Chapter 14 Fear

Fear is only a four-letter word but it is one of the most powerful words in our language. In one form or another, it seems to control most of us throughout our lives. It stops some of us from doing what we need to do and stops many of us from daring to be great. Worse still, it can paralyse people without them even knowing it.

If you start to understand the way fear impacts you at work, you become able to identify how fear holds you from doing what you need and want to do and how to break through your obstacles. You can start to unravel fear, work through it and stop allowing it to dominate you.

Fear is normal. People are affected by it to differing degrees and it will be more profound at certain times than others. Men and boys traditionally have had to tough it out and not admit to being fearful. But fear affects them just as much as it does women and girls. Type A personalities, egotists and hyperactive kids typically won't admit to it either.

No one escapes it. Like bullying, it often gets swept under the carpet. We don't talk about fear because we think we shouldn't have it and if we do, we're weak. And that's the problem: living like this stops us from being powerful. Imagine a hose that has little holes pricked into it. You can't see them but when you turn on the tap water is forced through those tiny holes. Fear is much the same. We can't see fear, so we think we can pretend it doesn't exist. But it does exist and it can have a huge impact on the way we do things.

You can make any number of excuses for not addressing workplace issues – too busy, too tired – but often the real underlying reason is *fear*. It's just masked in a myriad of ways. Moving through fear is difficult – it is challenging, confronting and that's why it is so often avoided.

It is up to *you*. You can choose to let fear hold you back or you can choose to move through your comfort zone and address the situations you have been avoiding. Think about it in terms of the business outcomes and what it is costing the organisation in lost productivity and profits. And remember to think about what it is costing *you*.

Take it on

To tackle it, to topple fear can be scary stuff but well worth the effort. Once you chip away at it – bit by bit – you can have the courage, confidence and ability to continue to work on it.

You will still experience fear (as everyone does) but you don't have to be captive to it. It may never be as easy as you'd like it to be, but you *can* do it. Be committed to developing yourself to the point where you are able to say I will do this – I will not be controlled by fear and then you've either *done it or you haven't*. Get someone on your team (a professional) who can help you to break through and to be courageous whilst you continue to reach your summits. So commit to action. You can look and act like a powerful leader.

What would you do if...?

When you're feeling fearful about a situation you have to manage, have a chat to yourself and ask: *What would I do if I felt confident in this situation? How would I handle it? How have I handled other situations I felt fearful of?* Then think about what you have done before that worked well and do it again. This process can help you to move through your roadblocks and to be effective even when you don't feel confident.

It takes time to be good at something and this process can help you to achieve a new level of confidence. *So fake it until you make it*, remaining calm and confident.

Nobody knows how you're feeling inside unless you tell them – so why would you bother? When people are not feeling self-assured they often put themselves down before starting something, even apologising in advance just in case they mess up. It's like having an each way bet. The only problem is that you're setting up the expectation that what you are about to say isn't worth hearing and effectively giving people permission to switch off from what you're saying. Therefore, in a sense you created the very outcome *you* feared.

Be brave, practice and they'll never know. Watch other influential leaders and emulate them. Whatever you do, *don't apologise* because it looks anything but powerful.

What does it look like?

Fear will look different for different people and in different situations. At the end of this chapter is a list of behaviours that people say they exhibit when fear is alive and well. Think about what you do when you are scared to do what you really want, then draw up a list. Many people find just by acknowledging and writing down their fears and the behaviours associated with them that it gives them a sense of relief. They learn how to strategically plan for the confronting situations where they would normally be inclined to let something or someone dominate them. They then become able to respond differently, in the manner they would have liked to behave previously because they learn how and then they practice, practice, practice until they're good at it.

Identified behaviours

- Being a people pleaser.
- Wanting to be one of the 'team'.
- Allowing situations to go on for longer than is advisable and kidding yourself that it's the right thing to do.
- Going along with the majority in meetings rather than saying what needs to be said.
- Letting cranky employees rule the roost.
- Not being committed to performance management.
- Feeling anxious and not in control.
- Not doing what you are employed to do.
- Worrying about what your peers think of you.
- Worrying about what your employees think of you.
- Not spending enough time thinking so that you actually know what you have to do.
- Getting 'stuck' in the thinking stage.
- Not spending time reviewing actions.
- Not taking time out to 'observe' what's really going on in your workplace.

SEX IN THE BOARDROOM

Avoid avoid

If you at times play the avoid game then you're not alone – we all do it. It's normal. This chapter is not referring to those situations when dealing with an issue is delayed on the odd occasion. It is referring to the delay of dealing with important issues put off time after time.

Becoming *aware* of when you are playing the avoid game is the first step toward stopping it. The next step is to think about what you actually need to do to resolve it. Set up a plan to achieve it and then *do* it.

Moving forward

When I am concerned about asking a client a tough question and wonder how they'll react, I hold myself accountable and think about what I should be doing to help the client to the greatest extent possible. I then decide what I should do and *do* it. I fake it until I make it. They are not aware I am nervous – that is my problem to overcome, not theirs. It is my responsibility to be honest and to ask specific questions when necessary – that is what my clients pay me to do so I must do it. My apprehension is my problem and they need never to know about it.

You can do the same. Notice what you need to do. Identify the outcomes for the business, your people and yourself. And do it. Make a mental note as to whether it was easy or hard and think about how you manage the process as you become more practiced at it.

Writing in your workbook and making mental notes can help you continue to move forward. It can help you to be a powerful leader, to act with integrity and to hold yourself true to your values.

Barrier identified

James, a senior manager, broke through his fear barrier by having the tough conversation he needed to have with an under-performing male employee. He didn't *want* to talk to him and had put the conversation off for two very long years. James kept talking to everyone else about it and updating them on what the person was doing – updating everyone but the person who needed to know and who was the only one who could change the situation. He felt stressed, anxious and drained by the shame of constantly talking about it without ever *doing* what he knew was needed. And the longer he left it, the harder and more unlikely it was that he would actually do it.

There never seemed to be the right time to speak to him. When he finally made himself do it and organised a meeting with him the perpetrator was stunned. He had no idea about what he was meant to have done. He demanded some evidence before he would accept that this really was *his* problem, so James provided the evidence. He couldn't believe it. He felt angry to think that he hadn't been told about it a long time ago and he felt embarrassed that everyone knew except him. He felt annoyed to think that he hadn't been given a chance to address the offending behaviour. Later, when he had time to think about it, he was willing to change his behaviour and he apologised for it. James also apologised to him for the way he managed the situation.

What a waste of energy this situation was to everyone involved in it. For two long years, the person who could address the problem knew nothing about it while people who didn't need to know about it had regular updates. That's enough to make anyone squirm. It undermines the leader's overall performance, damages their credibility and it certainly does nothing for the employee involved.

James isn't a bad leader, in fact he's a decent person and certainly would be in the switched-on category. He works tirelessly to provide his team with a great place to work and he has taken the organisation to heights not achieved before. He's always implementing systems that will improve the workplace culture and puts a lot of effort into empowering those he leads. An unintentional side effect of James being so caught up in keeping a positive environment and not wanting to cause waves is that he created the very festering, unpleasant situation that he'd tried so hard to prevent. He was so relieved when he had the courage to resolve this situation because he could then put his energy into other areas that needed his attention.

Like many, James was simply too scared to do what he was paid to do and that is to have those tough conversations when necessary and hold people accountable for their behaviour.

Summary

Fear controls many of us more than we care to admit but by confronting fear, over time it will hold less power over us. Although you may feel that you're the only one under fear's control, talking to others reveals that fear has also dominated their thinking and controlled their life in a range of ways. So you are not alone.

Fear can reduce powerful leaders to mediocrity and can allow others to control us. It's not easy to tackle because the seeds are sown very early in our life and try as we might to free ourselves from this burden, fear is a regular visitor which needs to be managed. So stand firm, face up to your fears and move forward in your role. Think about fear as just something else you have to manage in your daily life and as you reduce its power, watch your own power grow.

The questions at the end of this chapter can help you to unravel your own thoughts on fear. They will help you probe and really understand what is going on in this part of your life. If you get this right, many of the other challenges you face will seem easy. Add to this list and draw up your own. Be honest with yourself. Remember that everyone has it - it isn't right or wrong – it just *is*.

Questions

1. If you drew a picture of fear, what would it look like in your daily life at work?
2. What is fear stopping you from doing right now?
3. How often does fear stop you from doing what you want or need to do?
4. Has fear been around for a while or is it something that you have just noticed?
5. What specific things help you to move through it?
6. What specific things help you to stay trapped in it?
7. How do you feel when you let fear dominate you?
8. How do you feel when you break through and just do it?
9. What successes have you had?
10. How will you know when you are managing it rather than it is managing you?

Chapter 15
Fake it until You make it

SEX IN THE BOARDROOM

You are a leader. As such, you are expected to be perfect, no chinks in your armour, perfect in everything that you do, able to work continuously and not be fatigued, the magician who is able to pull rabbits out of hats time and time again, more powerful than a locomotive and able to leap tall buildings in a single bound. So it seems to me that you may well need to fake it quite often in your leadership role.

Even in the most difficult situations people look to the leader to have the skills to manage, to be in control and of course to be composed at all times. However unrealistic, this is what the role demands and if you intend to be a powerful leader, you will need to accept this and perform accordingly. Certainly you must not tell people it is all too hard or curl up in the foetal position crying for mama because you don't know what to do or something didn't go quite the way you planned.

The term *fake it until you make it* does not imply that you will be dishonest or lack authenticity. It means that you will choose to be an actor until you are competent and confident in specific areas. It means that you will be willing to do whatever it takes to achieve your desired growth. And once this growth has been attained you will move onto other areas until you have mastered those as well.

Switched-on?

Successful switched-on leaders strive for excellence in everything they do. They live their lives as though this is normal – as it is, for them – and they will always be ready to go to the next level as quickly as possible. They might assume that everyone lives their life this way, though of course the reality is that very few people stay this focused and committed.

The difference between the leader profile and others is that they will continue to put themselves in this situation because they thrive on moving forward in their life. They'd be bored going from day to day, week to week, year to year, just plodding along doing the same old thing. It would drive them crazy.

Case study

Joseph was in the right place at the right time and after a very brief interview was appointed to an executive position. He was delighted because this was the break he had been waiting for. Although not having the proper corporate experience and knowing that he would not have been short-listed for the position had it been advertised in the normal circles, he was grateful for this opportunity.

Once in the role, he often wondered what on earth he was doing and what he needed to do. There was no induction process and no one to ask about the history of the project because everyone with the right knowledge had left the company, so as a professional in this situation, he had to either sink or swim. Joseph knew that this was an amazing opportunity and there was no way he would fail. He was single minded about succeeding and there was no doubt that he would because he had the skills, knowledge and experience – he just needed to work out what they wanted and how he could fulfil what he was commissioned to do.

Fake it until you make it was Joseph's daily mantra for a long time. He faked it a lot until he had the necessary information. The people on his committees were high profile and he spent the meetings freaking out inside but outwardly exuding a calm, confident demeanour. It always surprised him when colleagues told him how calm and confident he was because it certainly was not how he felt inside. It was indeed a stressful time with little or no support, so he had to work it out for himself as he went along. He survived the steep learning curve after doing a lot of research and piecing everything together. He became confident, competent and successful in the role. A number of the businesses he worked with won awards and projects he started back then continue to this day. Looking back, Joseph realised that some of his colleagues knew he didn't have the corporate experience and although it did bother him initially, he knew there was nothing he could do about the past. One colleague in particular seemed to be compiling a dossier on him as to what he hadn't done in the corporate world. This made him even more determined to succeed at it. He was very grateful for the opportunity that this project gave him because it opened the door to many other opportunities and continues to do so. And he was grateful for the advice to fake it because it gave him freedom. Once he did that, he started soaring with the eagles and loved it.

Speaking of faking it

Confident people can become a quivering mess when they have to speak in public. It can bring on panic attacks and it's not uncommon for a leader to allow their subordinate to deliver the speech because they tell them it will be a good experience for them. You only have a few seconds to grab the audience's attention so the introduction needs to be truly powerful. Nerves can make people apologise, stutter and stammer which is not a good look when you're supposed to be a powerful leader.

You will need to be a polished presenter in many situations and if this is a challenge for you, then take it slowly. Identify what you are anxious about and work step by step to move through your fears. There are many courses, books and professionals who can help you to overcome your fear of public speaking.

Once you are good at it, you will have people in the palm of your hand and can take them on a journey. They will want to listen to you because you have done your research, you know what you are talking about and you are interesting. You are tuned into your audience and can sense when you need to change tack to hold their attention and to deliver what they want and need to hear about your topic. And when you need to change tack you do it seamlessly because you can.

Zip it

I coined the term *Zip It* model after I noticed that it is common for leaders to say what they are not good at rather than building themselves up. It's as if they're too scared to tell people what they're good at lest they be seen to be boasting or bragging.

They also seem to think they're the only ones with the negative voice in their heads, not realising that almost everyone shares that same experience every day. Few people can control the *thoughts* that zoom around in their head, but every single person with normal intelligence and mental health is in complete control of what comes out of their *mouth.*

Inappropriate behaviour

Michael, a team leader was verbally attacked by one of his colleagues in front of his people and others in the department. Neil lambasted him and let him know in no uncertain terms that he was not impressed about something he was supposed to have done. Michael was shocked and stood there in total disbelief. He felt like a fool in front of everyone and didn't respond or react because he didn't know what to do.

He didn't know how to handle this situation – then or after it had occurred. He thought about it for quite awhile and he was determined not to allow it to negatively impact him or to allow him to act like a wimp at work.

He knew that he wasn't responsible for the attack nevertheless it had happened and he had to deal with it. It was Neil's problem but he certainly felt it. Maybe he'd had a bad day? Whatever the reason, he bore the brunt of it at that moment. Some people apologise, others don't.

Faking it is a good idea until you can think about ways of responding. The way this team leader handled it was to just stand there and not react. He looked confident but certainly didn't feel it inside. He then discussed the situation with someone he trusted (a professional) who could help him to develop a plan to move through it.

After things cooled down he arranged to have a meeting with Neil and their manager to discuss the situation that had occurred. This took a lot of courage and he spent time planning the meeting before he scheduled it. It was a pleasant enough meeting and he was firm with his colleague. He told Neil that if there is an issue then he would appreciate it if he would make a time to meet with him and together they can work out the appropriate way to move forward. He informed him that although he understood these things happen, he was not going to allow such behaviour in the future.

This took a lot out of Michael and he felt proud of himself for having the courage to do it. It was a big step forward for him in his leadership development and style. He said that the fake it until you make it principle was what kept him focused while he was part of the meeting. It is never easy taking someone on and explaining to them why their behaviour is unacceptable.

Facilitating

Naomi was excited and thrilled to be invited to be the keynote speaker for an important annual event with an expected audience of over 200 women. One

Chapter 15 Fake it until You make it

of her goals at the time was to speak to a large group and this was her chance to do it.

She prepared thoroughly, knew what she would say, thought long and hard about what she would wear and did the appropriate research in order to deliver a presentation that would be powerful in every way, one that would make them want to get to know her and more about her business. She wouldn't have been so excited if she'd have known what an ordeal it was going to be.

The organisation had changed venues at the last minute and the business manager knew little about acoustics. Being a novice she didn't really know what to expect with microphones and how to set up the room for maximum impact of the presentation, so she just ran with how they had done it.

They placed the lectern where the audience could not see her easily. The microphone didn't work properly and the actual presentation that she was talking to was 30 feet away from her. Only the people closest to her could hear and the microphone only worked effectively when Naomi had her back to the audience. It also wouldn't allow her to move from the lectern, which was a real challenge because her natural inclination is to move through the audience. And to make it worse a group of executives at one table had had one drink too many and were vocal throughout the whole presentation.

Naomi could have fallen in a heap. She could have apologised over and over. But she refused to do that because she'd seen other presenters doing it, it doesn't look powerful in any sense of the term and you lose the audience's attention immediately. And it can take you weeks to get over the disaster rather than just to look at it for what it is – a learning experience and get on with what else you have to do.

It could have been an absolute disaster had she not decided there and then that she would make the most of it. It became Naomi's opportunity to give the audience the impression that she could handle any situation, no matter how difficult. And so she did. Fortunately for her she was also facilitating a workshop the next day and that gave her a chance to put her professionalism on show again and to deliver a powerful workshop.

Summary

Learning how to manage difficult situations and persisting with something until you have accomplished it builds your character, self-esteem and confidence. It's good for you. You have achieved something that arms you with the skills and courage to continue on to the next level and fulfil

Chapter 15 Fake it until You make it

your potential. There will be ups and downs and times when you may feel like giving up. But when you continue to push forward, mastering something that you'd previously felt was impossible, you start to realise that you can do whatever you want to do. It just takes time (perhaps a lot of it) and an absolute determination to not give up. And it gives you the confidence to try other things in which you may not yet be competent.

The benefit to you and to those you lead will be enormous. You will become a role model and mentor to others without even realising it. They will aspire to be like you and they will think that it is easy because you make it look that way. You will exude positive energy that reflects your commitment to excellence and they will respect you for that. You can choose to surround yourself with fantastic people who inspire and encourage you, to keep going for *gold*, to find the courage to do it and to never give up until you've achieved what you set out to do. There may well be quite a bit of faking it but that's okay because everyone who has ever been successful has done a lot of it.

Chapter 16
Bullying

Chapter 16 Bullying

It would be remiss of me to omit bullying in the workplace from a book on leadership. I'd feel as though I were not being ethical, pretending it doesn't exist and continuing a pattern that has been accepted at work and in general society for a very long time. But anyone who has ever had anything to do with people knows that bullying does happen and it happens a lot. In some cases bullying might be just an annoyance but in other cases the experience can be much worse than that. It can have a serious impact in the workplace and on its inhabitants. And it's not gender specific. Both sexes are very good at it. Although illegal in many countries it is something that continues to thrive, often aided and abetted.

There are many forms of bullying and I'm sure you have experienced it too either as a victim or protagonist and that between us, we could write a whole book just on this subject.

Flavours

Have you ever seen an overt bully in action? This is the one who bullies everyone, doesn't care who knows it and nobody dares stand up to them. Even the boss finds it difficult to manage the situation. This can lead to complex and troubled dynamics. For such overt and confident bullying to exist, the staff member in question may well be friends with someone higher in the organisation and when tackled about their inappropriate behaviour, they may call on the influence of this more senior person. Or they may think they are within their rights and they are not going to be perturbed by anyone at all. These bullies need to be tackled and sorted out. They make other people's lives a misery simply because they can.

Some bullies have learnt the art of subterfuge: they bully those around them but toady up to the boss. The boss never sees the bullying behaviour first-hand, so finds it hard to believe that bullying really is taking place. As soon as the boss walks in the door these bullies switch to displaying the charming side of their persona. The manager wonders how anyone could possibly have a problem with someone who is always so pleasant and for whom nothing is too much trouble.

Sometimes a bully is not aware of their behaviour and if challenged will completely reject any notion that they've done something wrong. *I've always behaved like this and I'm not going to change now.* It's not bullying, *it's just a bit of fun and they need to get over it. If you can't have fun at work then what is this world coming to? It's about you, not me. It's political correctness gone nuts.* These bullies can be unrelenting and aggressive and you will have your work cut out for you if they are part of your team.

Few people will take lightly to being told they're a bully. When dealing with someone without enough emotional intelligence to recognise that their behaviour is bullying and that it does affect their workmates, be prepared for a difficult, long process. Be careful with your language to improve the likelihood of them actually hearing what you have to say. Try using different words to avoid getting their back up but don't allow their aggression to dominate you or to stop you from doing what you have to do. You could link necessary changes to their performance review. Help them to understand their behaviour is unacceptable and although it may be 'normal' for them, society has moved on and expects people to be more respectful.

Policy

Most large organisations and public sector departments have a formal written policy on bullying; if you don't have one then get cracking on developing it now. Making a difference in this insidious behaviour is important to current and future generations of workers.

Unfortunately most companies keep their bullying policy locked away safe and sound in a cupboard somewhere and don't activate it even when they know bullying is happening. People don't want to get involved in the problem and they hope it will go away. It won't. Confirm that your organisation has a policy and make it clear that you are willing to use it against bullies.

Educate yourself and educate your people because it is rare to find a workplace where bullying is not happening in one form or other. Humans are not perfect and behaviours from the schoolyard find their way into the workplace. Remember you are not their parent so you might need to educate yourself about how to educate adults in this sensitive area.

Alert new staff to what you will and won't accept right at the outset. At their induction, make it clear that bullying is unacceptable and discuss what you mean by bullying. It may be useful to include refreshers in development workshops a couple of times a year to confirm that your place of business has a total ban on any form of bullying.

Case study

I accepted a job with someone who was very charming, with a real air of authority and success about him. I was actually quite excited about it, because even though I was more highly qualified than him, I thought he would be a great mentor because of his experience.

Chapter 16 Bullying

It didn't take long for the charming façade to dissipate. He used unpredictability to control. I went from being a strong and confident program director to being jumpy and nervous. I still did a great job in the role, but I was never sure about what was going to be acceptable and what was going to set him off.

I'd discuss a proposed plan with him, he'd change it, wait until I'd told clients and sponsors, then change it back to what I'd suggested in the first place. Then I'd have to look like a fool and go back to the clients and sponsors to tell them the plan had changed.

We could have had all morning to talk together, but he would wait until I was grabbing my keys and on my way out and suddenly something would become so important that couldn't wait – so I'd be late for a meeting and look rude and inconsiderate.

Then to cap it off, we changed the strategic plan because the one that was in place when I started really wasn't going to work. I implemented it to perfection and got fantastic reviews from the various parties involved. When it came to performance review time, guess what? The official KPIs on my contract were those that were linked to the old strategic plan and hadn't been changed to reflect the new strategic plan, so even though I'd done an amazing job and exceeded the requirements of the strategic plan, he had an excuse to turn down the bonus because I hadn't met the old, redundant KPIs. Given that the pay was structured so that the bonus was about half my pay, that was quite a nasty thing to do. Having half a year on half pay was a bitter pill to swallow. He did things like that just because he could. He didn't care in the least. He'd come back from General Manager (GM) meetings ranting about the two female GMs, how being over forty and childless had turned them into bitter, twisted women and how it was his goal to ruin their careers in such a way that they would know it was him but would never be able to prove it. I stuck out the job for a year to the day. He was sacked six weeks later but that was too late for me. It took me a good two years to properly recover from that experience and lose the fear and jumpiness with my new boss. Louise

Case study

Simon was *old-school* and led his team with a big stick. He thought of himself as a kind and caring senior executive who followed company policy and procedure to the letter. When he had to discipline staff or have a tough conversation, he would treat his staff like naughty children. Everything in his manner told them how naughty they had been. Simon would have the particular policy in front of him, read it verbatim from the manual, humiliating the staff member in front of their peers. He would ask them if they understood what they'd done wrong and get them to sign a statement saying that they would never again do whatever it was that they did. Then they'd be sent back to their workstation. And if the employee did do it again, Simon simply repeated the same procedure all over again.

He followed this approach for a long time, assuming that it must be working because no one argued with him. In reality it wasn't working at all. It took him a long time but eventually he noticed that staff turnover was high, morale was low, absenteeism was much higher than the industry average, productivity was low, his department was not meeting their monthly goals and he rarely had a pleasant conversation with any of his team. He had no idea about the impact of his behaviour. He was following instructions from his manager and because he worked in a global corporation he thought they must have had the experience and know how to develop policy that was *right*.

Unease

For the most part people are unsure about what to do when they see someone being bullied. They are concerned they may themselves be seen as the baddy, get used as a scapegoat or victimised for their troubles, while the bullying only gets worse. Support may be scant, with colleagues being afraid to intervene in case they become the new target. This concern is well founded and reflects the experience of many who have been courageous enough to bring it to their manager's attention. The old-school attitude to bullying in the workplace can be to write someone off as being weak if they complain. *We never used to worry about it, you're just soft now and can't handle the pressure. Just get on with it.*

It's very difficult to *just get on* with bullying in the workplace. It's systemic. Everyone the victim associates with is affected as well, either through trying to give support, or through dealing with the guilt of their own inaction if they are too afraid to speak out against what is happening. And it doesn't stop there. Bullying in the workplace can often have an impact on other areas of the person's life.

It's not something that should be taken lightly. It can make people's life difficult but much worse than that it can destroy lives. Bit by bit it can erode someone's self-esteem and confidence until they feel as though they can't take it anymore, particularly when they're told to just get over it and *stop being a girl.* It is difficult to weed out bullies, to hold them accountable for their actions and to assist those who have been victims of this behaviour, but do it you must.

Given that bullies generally have low self-esteem when they are brought to account it seems like an oxymoron to me that even confident, strong, intelligent people allow bullies so much power. Most bullies roll over when they are brought to justice and just like dogs, want their belly scratched. They seem to be desperate for approval.

Case study

Vicky and Troy sat on the board of an organisation but in different groups. During a get together for the organisation, Vicky went to Troy and informed him that she was very disappointed that he hadn't been doing enough for her group and hoped he would remedy this situation as soon as possible. Vicky was rude, loud and obnoxious and went on and on. Troy said little, being shocked at this attack and where it occurred. He was staggered that someone would behave like this at a function when everything was supposed to be fun and lighthearted. Troy went overseas shortly after this and was unable to contact anyone because of the holiday break. When he returned he spoke to key people about what had happened. The situation dragged on for months because no one returned phone calls and in the end Troy felt like he was the bully because he wanted to make sure that the situation was resolved and Vicky couldn't behave like this with other people in the organisation. Whilst he could move on, he knew that not everyone could handle bullies and just get on with it.

Eventually the relevant people met. They had

done their research and found that other people thought Vicky could be a bit full-on and difficult, but their own experience was that they could just tell her to behave and she would. Management decided that it was Troy's problem and that he had overreacted because he was tired, stressed and in need of a holiday. Troy decided to let the situation go because it was causing more problems that it was worth – he valued these people because of the brilliant work they were doing with the rest of the organisation and he wanted to get on with enjoying his time as a board member.

Sometime later, Vicky and her team organised an international event and Troy heard on the grapevine that Vicky was driving everyone nuts – she was bullying them, she was a control freak, abusing them for not doing enough or for not doing it her way, intimidating them the whole time the event was being planned. After the conference a number of committee members resigned.

Troy knew that the people in charge would have been advised about this behaviour so in the long-term they would have found out that Troy had in fact told the truth – Vicky was a bully. This bullying behaviour had continued because no one wanted to 'cause waves' and to tell Vicky that her behaviour was unacceptable and to hold her accountable for it. And because of this a lot of unnecessary suffering occurred with many people – not just Troy.

Case study

Leeane had an interesting experience some years ago when she took on a role she felt passionate about but it was at a much lower job grade than she really was. She loved the sound of the role and the work she'd be doing so Leeane decided to apply for it and was hired. As a result of this reduction in status, Leeane learnt about another dimension to bullying and human behaviour that she hadn't come across before in the workplace.

What she found was that one person high up in the organisation only saw her job grade and treated her accordingly. The business manager had no idea about what else Leeane did but she'd obviously decided that the job grade meant that she was not that important and she treated her that way. Leeane put up with it for a while but eventually she knew it had to stop because the manager was way out of line.

After 'the final straw' had occurred and the manager said one nasty thing too many, Leeane let her know clearly that she didn't like the way she was being treated and she needed to treat her with respect. After that day, she never bothered her again and they just ignored each other. They looked in different directions when they passed each other in the corridor. Leeane said she still had butterflies in her stomach when she saw her but just faked it and looked totally uninterested because she was not going to allow her to intimidate her anymore. Leeane said the manager looked nervous and this surprised her.

Summary

We know that bullying won't ever be completely wiped out – there will always be someone trying to dominate another but what we do have in our favour is knowledge about how bullying impacts on workplaces and on people in general. It is your moral and legal responsibility to do something about bullies in your workplace, to whatever extent you are able. If there's an issue, let's fix it now. Treat it like any other organisational issue that has to be resolved. You can educate your employees and keep your eyes and ears open and become aware of all the forms of bullying that can occur. Know that it can happen where any group of people are together and that it is most probably happening in your workplace in some form, though it can indeed be subtle and you may miss it. Let your people know that whilst you aren't perfect you will do your utmost to stomp on bullying as soon as you become aware that it is happening. This is real leadership, powerful leadership: taking a stand, not 'sweeping it under the carpet' as previous generations have done and as many still do even now in the 21st century.

Chapter 16 Bullying

Chapter 17
Holidays

SEX IN THE BOARDROOM

Insight

Each time I go on holidays, in addition to planning for them, I also have to prepare my thoughts; otherwise I stay in work mode and do not enjoy the break because I keep checking emails and answering the business mobile. I need to be kind to myself, be patient like I am with others and start to identify what I really want to do so that I can feel relaxed. I need to let my passion and enthusiasm replace tiredness, exhaustion and the occasional cynical thoughts that have crept in to my mind. It takes me a good week to unwind and it can be a horrible time. Nevertheless I take the time out and I do what I enjoy because I want to come back to work feeling refreshed and able to achieve great things with those I lead and for the business in general.

Chapter 17 Holidays

The busier the leader the more likely they are to be bad at taking time out from work. If a holiday is actually taken, then it will just be a quickie with one eye on the clock, the other checking email on the laptop. It's not necessarily that the leader thinks themselves important, irreplaceable or that people can't manage without them. It's probably because they haven't actually thought about it. They haven't stopped long enough to think about the ramifications of this behaviour upon themselves, their business or on their long-term productivity.

Taking holidays is hard when you've been very busy because it's actually really hard to just stop one day and be expected to relax, unwind, enjoy and take it easy. If this is you, think about: what would happen if you died? What would happen if you were so ill that you couldn't work? What would the people calling you in your holiday do then? Would they know how to make a decision without you? Would the business survive without you? And what would everyone do if you left this role and took another job?

Real holidays

When I say *holidays*, I mean getting as far away as you can afford to go and doing what you love to do. Things that make you feel great inside and that

SEX IN THE BOARDROOM

invigorate you.

I don't mean having a day off here, a day off there or having the odd long weekend away. Nor am I referring to having a holiday and working around the home or getting caught up in family dramas. You need a real break. It doesn't matter what that break is as long as it is what really works for *you*. You might enjoy being active and trying new things or you might just want to lie around and relax and read books. Whatever you do is fine, so long as it has the desired result.

Plan for them

You can use the same principle to plan for your holiday as you do for your personal weekly meeting. Draw up a timeline and write down exactly what you want to do. Many people don't bother to do the plan and end up just hanging around the house and working. Then before they know it they're back at work.

Get as far away as you can. Get away from your mobile (turn it off), take a different mobile just for family and friends, stay away from the laptop (hide it) and away from anyone who wants you for work related issues (act dumb). Don't leave an auto-reply email message telling them that you are on holidays and that if it's *urgent* they can contact you on your mobile number because their definition of urgent may be quite different from what the real word means. Leave someone else's number or if you don't have anyone to whom you can delegate then leave the date of your return and promptly respond to them when you return from your fantastic break. It doesn't matter what position you are in the company, it will survive without you. If you didn't work because you'd moved on, were retrenched or were dead, they'd have to manage without you and in a way you are helping your organisation to develop a succession plan. If something happens they will have to manage so think about the leadership development opportunities you're giving them.

Relaxing
Some people don't know how to relax because they're so fired up. They need to learn. They can observe what other people do to unwind and relax. They can talk to other people to discover what they do to enjoy themselves away from work. If they're really stuck they can listen to other people's conversations (even when they're not meant to) about what the conversationalists did on the weekend, on holiday or what they love doing in their spare time. There are also many television programs to give you ideas. Books on the subject abound and it's worth reading

some of these books because they suggest many different things to do and one or more of these may end up being hobbies for you.

Set the goal of having an outstanding holiday. Identify what that means to you at this time and then plan for it to happen. Keep in mind that sometimes things happen you don't count on when you're on a break and if this does occur, don't throw your hands up in the air and say – I knew this would happen, do other things, just don't sit around and feel rotten. However, if all goes well and you can do as you planned, try new things and see what you enjoy doing.

Lindsay's story
Lindsay is a decent leader who cares about his people, puts their interests in front of his own and just gets on with the job of managing. He continues to work tirelessly for the business without having adequate holidays or breaks but ensures his staff have their annual holidays and all other entitlements. He'd never dream of expecting them to work 12 hour days, weekends or on public holidays. He can't remember the last time he had a decent holiday – just days off here and there and he always works on weekends. When he does have time off he's mowing the lawn or taking his kids to their various

activities. He also finds time for his wife because he is a committed family man and his family is very important to him.

He first worked with me to find out why he had lost his passion. He was wary of the process and didn't want to waste his time so he checked it out before he decided to do any leadership development. When we first met he looked weary. He looked as though he hadn't been in the sun for a very long time and he looked very, very tired. He wasn't dressed the way he should have been for his level of seniority and the way he spoke indicated he was burnt-out, sick and tired of work and wondered whether he should just move on. He wondered why he had lost his enthusiasm for the job and that each day just felt like the next. He said he used to be passionate about his role but doesn't feel it these days.

Back from holidays

It might not be until you actually return from holidays that you realise how worn out you were prior to your departure. And it might take you a little while to get back into it at work. Take it easy, you'll rev up quickly enough and before you know it another year will be gone and you'll be due for holidays again.

Record the useful bits of your holiday before you get into this pace again. Write down what worked for you in your workbook and how you found ways of enjoying yourself and what relaxing meant for you. Back at work it's easy to forget what you did last holidays that made such a difference.

People often comment that the stress, anxiety and worries they had prior to going on holidays, the fear and concern about all of the stuff they had to do disappeared over the period they were away and they come back with renewed energy and focus. They stop just doing things and ensure they have a strategic plan they follow to achieve the business outcomes and that they are not busy for the sake of it. The holiday has given them the confidence to be innovative and to get moving with plans they know will make a huge difference to the longevity of the organisation.

Chapter 17 Holidays

Case study

Ayla wasn't used to taking holidays and couldn't work out whether to take seven days, 14 days or the full month. She decided she'd play around with the time she took off and see how she felt when she came back to work to help her decide what would be the best timeframe for her to have off each break.

Her experiment revealed that seven days was not anywhere long enough. She found that she hardly had time to relax before she was back at it again. Next time she took 14 days off and she found a similar thing occurred. Whilst this certainly was better than seven days, she found that the break still didn't allow her to have her 'down time'. She had lots to do with the family and she had many jobs to do around the home. Ayla noticed she also started to think about work a few days before her holidays ended. She decided the next holiday would be longer and she would then review how it worked. She felt that it would be useful to put the relevant details in her workbook so that she could record her findings from previous holidays knowing that by the time the holiday came around she'd probably have forgotten about these powerful insights. What she did find very useful was to turn the mobile off but she was in a quandary because it was the only one she had and so she had to decide what messages she would respond to and which ones she wouldn't which still kept her connected to work on her break. Ayla also decided rather than worry about work before coming back to it that in her plan she could identify the specific timeframe when she would sit down and decide what she needed to do and that it could be on the weekend before she returned or she could allocate time on the first day to do it.

Best practice

Managers work hard and most are concerned about the people they lead, often looking after their people better than they look after themselves. They expect employees to take breaks, to take holidays, to get sick pay and to access the many other benefits they're entitled to. Think about the unspoken message this sends to the employees. If you're an employer of choice who really cares about their people and who insists on employees working regular hours, not taking work home or working on weekends then it's even worse. *Do as I say - not as I do*. What part of this fits best practice?

Research shows clearly that when senior management have fantastic policies in place but don't walk the talk, then employees are often reticent about utilising them because they are concerned that doing so may result in backlash from senior management and their fellow workers. Working hard and taking holidays are not at opposite ends of the same scale. If you take your holidays when they are due each year, it won't detract from your performance at work, it will enhance it.

Summary

Taking regular breaks and holidays throughout the year is one of the keys to being able to stay on top of things. They re-energise you; they allow you to gather your thoughts and they allow you to get yourself back on-track so that you come back to work refreshed and enthusiastic for the coming year.

If you are far more diligent about making sure your people have a break than you are for yourself, you need to remember that those you lead follow your example. Think about the message you send to your people if you don't subscribe to taking annual holidays.

If you work for an organisation which doesn't allow for the fact that you are not a machine and can't physically or mentally work 24x7 then you might want to show the senior team the research that shows how much an under-performing manager costs a typical organisation. Then show them the reams of evidence supporting the proposition that to truly perform at your peak, you need a healthy life away from work and time when you genuinely can relax and do what refreshes your mind and body.

SEX IN THE BOARDROOM

If the information in this chapter hasn't made you realise just how important regular uninterrupted breaks and holidays are to your overall performance as a leader and you haven't scheduled in your diary as to when you will take your next vacation then you're probably long overdue for a stress check and a long, long holiday. Think of your holidays as part of your health insurance and know that to get a good return you will have to invest quite a bit.

Questions

1. When did you have your last holiday?
2. Was it uninterrupted by work commitments?
3. Do you ensure your people have holidays uninterrupted by work?
4. How much effort went into planning your holiday?
5. For how long did you go away?
6. What did you do?
7. How long did it take you to unwind?
8. How did you feel at the end of the holiday?
9. How did you feel about going back to work?
10. How different did you feel after having a well-earned rest?

Chapter 18
Globalisation

SEX IN THE BOARDROOM

Insight

When you have geographically separated teams working for you, you could be the odd-one out initially. They work together and *they* have the connection. It's like a group of kids in the playground – they won't necessarily want the new kid to join in without proving themselves first and they certainly won't want the new kid to spoil their fun. The problem with this scenario is that you are the new kid *and* you are the boss. You have to work out how to lead effectively, be respected and retain the right level of control because regardless of which play-ground these 'kids' are in, they're supposed to help you achieve your targets.

The good news is that as a leader in the 21st century you now have dozens of ways you can connect with your globally dispersed people that were not available to your predecessors. Globalisation isn't new – it's the speed with which it is happening that is mind boggling. You can't afford to be complacent. Be aware of the difficulties you can face, be innovative, make strong connections with those on the ground, learn and understand the difference in cultural expectations and remember there will probably be even more things to think about next week. That way you will have a better chance of executing your management responsibilities more effectively.

Working internationally is a great opportunity to extend yourself as a leader. Your leadership style will influence the level of success you achieve. If you go in with an arrogant attitude, they'll be ready to enjoy the spectacle of you coming unstuck. So be patient and tolerant, be understanding of differences and willing to go that extra mile for your people. This will set you up for respect and reciprocated tolerance for the mistakes you will almost inevitably make because of language or cultural differences and other challenges.

Experience will always be a great teacher, but there are many things you can do to stop learning from trial and error. Hindsight is always illuminating but it is far better to learn from other people's mistakes so you make fewer mistakes in the first place. Over time you will no doubt draw up your own list of successes and things to be avoided at all costs.

Uniqueness of each country

Many companies still make the big mistake of assuming that their proven capability to manage will mean they can handle geographically dispersed teams easily. They underestimate the importance of the culture. To maximise productivity and profits, the people responsible for that region need to stay committed and satisfied. This can only happen if an organisation is open to the way that locals do things.

Even to the most casual of observers, the USA, Japan, India and the Middle Eastern countries are obviously different from each other. But within regions and within individual countries quite distinct cultures can exist. Take the Middle East for instance. The UAE is wildly different to Saudi Arabia. Similarly within India, the culture differs greatly depending on whether you are in the north, south, east or west.

I think there are four important things that are crucial for a chance to be successful in managing teams located in different countries. First, one has to be fully aware of the prevalent culture in the target country, like acceptable working hours and eating habits.

Second is to remember that the world is increasingly polarised on religion and hence it is important to consider religious beliefs. For example in the month of Ramadan, irrespective of one's own religion, in Muslim countries, one is not allowed to eat at all in the office or public in the day and some places don't even allow water intake.

Third is to be politically aware. Some countries do not tolerate any kind of jokes from any member of the organisation.

And finally, language. I recall, three years ago, expatriates in countries like Kazakhstan found it impossible to even read road signs without knowing Russian. It is impossible to contribute in such an environment without knowing the local language. So, one would attempt to hire local employees for positions.

Overall, one needs to understand that the 'one size fits all' equation does not work, or that the market entry success formula for one country cannot be the same for another. As long as the company's top management is clear about that, they would have a higher success probability. Abhay

Future planning

The leadership structure of today is not necessarily what you may need in the future. Remember everything is changing and changing fast. If you do not have the necessary talent and leadership in the local base, envision the dream team you need and create it. Imagine what your organisation is supposed to look like and shift the balance according to your business. If 60% of your customers are in Asia, your organisation needs to reflect this reality. You then need to reverse-engineer to where you need to be in the near future.

Dig into your current organisation at regional levels. Identify individuals with talent, drive and the ability to be coached and mentored. Try to place them in positions where they can grow. These individuals must be able to work across cultures and geographic regions.

Find people in the organisation who have the flexibility to move to different countries, who can learn by becoming truly local and leave an impression behind. Make it their job to replace themselves. Remember that you will also need to provide a vision of what they will be doing at the end of their overseas assignments, otherwise they mightn't be keen on being replaced.

Use expatriates in a non-traditional manner.

Chapter 18 Globalisation

I am a strong believer in rotational assignments. Place your best and brightest people in the local environment for a year or more and provide them with on the job training. For example, a European manager could move to Singapore and may eventually decide to become a Singaporean employee. You can retain the same European salary level and everyone wins because the manager is challenged to have a broader, bigger impact.

Set performance benchmarks and mechanisms in place to both motivate and evaluate your people. Provide feedback, then identify the star performers that you don't want to lose under any circumstances and make them part of your dream team. Spend 70% of your time with A-ranked performers, 30% with your B performers and systematically weed out non-performers.

Motivate your international team by inviting them to participate in the decision making process. Some people are naturally driven so give these high performers opportunities to learn and grow. Others want to be in the spotlight. At the end of the day, everyone works to earn a living. Why do we stay in one place? For most people, it is because they see a future that lines up with their hopes and dreams. Clearly, a manager plays a critical role in articulating an employee's career path with the company. When employees do not have that clarity in mind, they might leave.

Managing international teams requires three key elements. Place your team close to your customer base, hire key employees locally, so they can build their own—and the organisation's—future. Envision your dream team and create a step by step plan to get there, acquire, develop and retain diverse talents to build a high performance team to set the pace for everyone in the organisation and use a structured approach to planning and execution. Be clear on objectives and implement methodologies that enable quick feedback to workers. Suresh

Chat room

A simple, yet effective way to connect all of your employees is to have a chat room on-line. Rather than many private conversations occurring between team members, group discussions can help people to be part of a group and this system enables teams to feel much less isolated.

Case study

The main barriers to working with my teams globally have been the language and cultural differences. I have found it useful to provide training on cultural differences. Learning about these differences allows you to know how someone from another culture will react on certain things. Do we have to give orders before action is taken? Is it better to copy a boss in an email to get some action? Do we have to meet each other first and have a meal together before we can actually start working? Does the tone we use in our voice need to be formal or is it preferable to be a bit informal?

What should be not dependent on location is the progress report. There are many tools available on the market to make global communication easier. The main ones are email and teleconferencing but I have used NetMeeting / WebEx / LiveMeeting a lot. In addition, things like eRoom for document exchange can be beneficial. Ideally, I would like to see every team member at least once during a project, preferably at the start of the project but travel is not always possible. Serge

Virtual teams

I have managed virtual global teams for a long time, starting well before the internet era and some of the lessons learned back then are still valid today. I have found that the communications aspect is fundamental to any successful management and even more so for international management. One of the keys is to speak several languages.

In the corporation I worked for at the time it was a requirement to be fluent in at least three languages to be eligible for a management position at corporate headquarters. Even though the corporate language was English, speaking several languages helped tremendously. All team members used English words, however pronunciation was heavily coloured by the mother tongue and sometimes to a degree that the words were hardly recognisable as such. When you have experienced the challenges of doing business in a foreign language, you know you need to use very simple English and try to stay away from slang and idioms so you know the people you're working with don't feel stupid because they can't understand you.

I have become more sensitive to what language teachers call false friends, meaning similar sounding words from another language or literal translations have a different meaning in another language. If you have never struggled with this yourself, it can cause a lot of angst for everyone before you become aware of what is happening.

Citizens from any country need to realise that when they have to manage an international team out of their native country they need to educate themselves about the country they're working in and this is easily done by reading some foreign newspapers and listening or watching broadcasts from abroad. Today with the internet it is even easier and inexpensive to learn and understand foreign cultures. I give this advice as I have worked for many international companies and have seen the damage managers can cause when they are stuck in their own centric view. Christian

Global teams
I believe that location really does not matter. It's a block we create. Teams irrespective of their locations can have clear deliverables. The leadership needs to develop a plan as to how they will manage the whole process. The number one factor that should not be missed is that in the era of globalisation, many countries attract as a destination due to local cultural, country, region specific drivers. It may be cost, availability of talent or regulatory support. While defining the team expectation, align your expectation to the driver that attracted your organisation to place work at that location. Joseph

Build bridges – not barriers
You need to find ways in which to build bridges and not barriers. I spent 20 years in corporate life based in Europe, Asia and the USA; working in and later leading globally dispersed teams. Nowadays I work as a consultant with my client teams similarly dispersed. From my perspective there are four

things I found useful when working with teams dispersed globally.

First and foremost, the importance of paying attention to the significance and value of apparently insignificant gestures, for example: picking global team colleagues up at the airport and not expecting them to catch public transport. Calling for a social chat when you have five minutes to spare and not just when it's about business. With my consulting clients I always bring a box of Scottish shortbread to the meetings. It has got to the stage whereby people in the Paris office know that I am in the building because the shortbread is there. This type of patterning activity builds the bridges and connectivity that endures between meetings.

Second, maximising the inter-connectivity of the team is critical and in leading a globally diverse and highly successful account management team, delegation of responsibility and accountability was one of the key tools. That way the team is empowered to make its own strategy happen as opposed to 'waiting for somebody else to do something'. Empowerment is one of the few devices that I know that actually overcomes inertia.

Cultural similarities are the building blocks of globally diverse teams. Often what makes a Japanese person tick is the same as what makes a Brit or an American or a Frenchman tick. Equally, what frustrates or alienates them can be the same negative behaviours. People are people first and of different nationalities a long way second. Once the bridges are found, it is important to keep them maintained and not surprisingly, well travelled bridges appear to need less maintenance. The problem is that it is too easy to focus on the differences and to see them as barriers to communication. In my experience people all over the world respect and enjoy fairness, family, friendship and fun.

Shared ownership is the third important factor: shared design and execution of the strategic plan. I expect each individual to contribute their particular knowledge and expertise and to take responsibility for leading the design of their particular section.

The goals must be aligned: 50% team goals, 50% personal goals. They don't get their full bonus without the team achieving their goals. Individual goals are entirely within the remit of the individual concerned and therefore this maintains their personal motivation. The individual objectives are of course aligned with the team strategy.

Finally, I ensure team-based feedback loops happen via regular reviews and discussions on strategic progress. It is less about 360 degree analysis, instead much more about sustained performance and I held regular discussions on the business objectives and the lessons learnt by each person. The key to making all three of these processes work is a leader who is committed to their own personal accountability as well as the team's objectives and the objectives of each and every individual within the team. It is one situation where most certainly the leader has to walk the talk. Hamish

Summary
Your commitment to engaging multilaterally and to doing what works will be significant in achieving your organisational goals. It will be an alliance shaped by your common goal. Technology can help you to connect with your people but primarily it will be your attitude, skills and knowledge that dictate whether you sink or swim.

People are people. Wherever they are, they have basic needs to be met. Your role is to be fair, firm and to be clear about what you want and need to achieve. Your people need to learn what you expect from them and how they can achieve your desired outcomes. Awareness of cultural differences is paramount and communicating with them in a way they understand is essential.

You need people on the ground with whom you speak regularly and who are able to ensure your projects are undertaken with ease. Adapting your style to suit those you lead and the country you are working in will assist you to manage the changing face of your business. Ensure you do your research prior to entering the market to prevent wasting significant time in fix it mode which ultimately erodes the profits of your business. Rushing in and demanding your team do what you say is unlikely to work and it is much more likely to create resistance and cause lower productivity.

Review your policies regularly. Keep on top of trends in all of the regions in which you work. This will ensure your decisions are informed. Identify and analyse reasons for any deterioration in performance and establish a strategic plan to change ineffective procedures.

When you integrate technology, talent, operations, finance, marketing along with investors, clients, partners you can assist your people to continue to meet organisational growth and objectives. Even if they are working well don't stop there. Continue to think about how you can do a better job and bring a greater return for your business.

As a leader there's never a time to become complacent. It's your role and responsibility to look to the future and to measure just how successful and effective you are in each of your responsibilities.

Chapter 19
The Long & Short of it

SEX IN THE BOARDROOM

Insight

You need the heart and you need the brain; effective leaders are those who get the right balance in using those two body parts. Rick

Chapter 19 The Long & Short of it

An erudite leader not committed to leadership development is unlikely to assist their organisation and people to go from strength to strength. Rather it is likely they will continue to attain more of what they don't want. Successful leaders know that being well read is only one component to powerful leadership. When a systematic process is adhered to, you can be a leader who is admired for their capability, authenticity and ability to lead powerfully because it's clear you know what you are doing and you have the results to show.

You may be the new kid in town or you may be a seasoned leader. It really doesn't matter where you're placed on the corporate ladder because there is always so much more to learn. The first thing you have to do is to get your act together because you can't be effective if you are mediocre in the way you lead, with your attitude or with the behaviour you demonstrate.

I wrote *Sex in the Boardroom* to guide, encourage, inspire and to empower you to stop, sit down, think and to audit your systems and processes. Then and only then can you identify what's working well and what the 'gaps' are. It is expected the various chapters of the book will give you the information you need to challenge yourself, to recognise what you're doing well, to acknowledge your successes and to have your eyes open for areas you can fine-tune and improve. The book has enough information, tips and ideas to transform your organisation, yourself and those you lead if you're willing to do the required work. You need to be proud of your achievements because that helps you to keep striving for excellence and to get through any bad patches.

The possibilities are endless with this type of work. You start working with yourself and your people. You help them unravel what's really happening and step by step you all forge ahead. Everyone starts focusing on what has to be done, they get their systems and processes in place, managers give their people clear, direct instructions and each person stops wasting time on things that don't make a difference. They are specific and strategic, the whole team knows what has to be done and they just *get on with it*. They do what they've been hired to do: think, plan, develop, get into action, measure what they have done to see how effective it *really* is. They tweak what needs tweaking. Everyone works towards the common goal and they know their role in the scheme of things. There is nothing better than seeing a workplace function like this. It looks like a well-oiled machine in operation.

Leadership is exciting. The better you get at it,

the more confident you become and the more you'll want to experiment with what you're doing. You will always be learning what you could do better and once confident, you can trial new things out just because you can. There is no ego, there's just hard work to find out what you're doing effectively. Leaders don't allow whinging – they expect their people to be part of the solution.

Being in management is not for the faint hearted, for those who don't like people or who can't sustain the constantly changing face of business. But it can be fantastic and that's why those who love it keep doing it even with all the obstacles they face. Leaders use their intellect to foster change and to implement great policies and procedures that really do work in the workplace.

Everything you do must be well thought out. There's no room for action without thinking and planning. Take regular time out to think, plan and review and do a major re-think at least every 12 months. Keep the lines of communication open between senior management and employees. Let everyone work towards one goal – that is to achieve outstanding business success year in and year out.

Successful leaders may fake it when required but they don't just jump head first into new territory without doing their homework. They know *what* the likely impact will be of any proposed changes and they know *how* they will sell it to those people who will have to put it in place. They have a contingency plan and are always monitoring results, ready to change pace and direction when it is necessary. And just as you learn to acknowledge yourself when things are going well, if you have teams who are under-performing then you must take responsibility for that too. As the leader you'll have to wear the good bits and the bad bits. You are It.

I never tire of working in the leadership development area. My passion and enthusiasm never wanes because when people are serious about the way they lead, the changes are evident within a short period of time. I work with all types of leaders – textbook and others. From my perspective I have the best job in the world. I see the way management can influence their whole organisation when they are focused and switched-on. There's nothing better than seeing this in action with everyone working together – they are each part of the jigsaw and it all fits together beautifully.

We'd all love our personal assistant to present us each day with our To Do List. If you don't have one, you'll have to do it yourself because being organised is a big part of success. Having your head spin with 'where is this' or 'what do I have to do' is unhelpful. Make room for interruptions but stay on task. Don't let other people's agendas dominate you, because that is effectively choosing to get on a treadmill. Pushing yourself too hard won't achieve powerful results because anyone who works themselves to the bone performs below par in the long run.

Just as you need to have your finger on the pulse each day in the workplace you need to be aware when it's the right time to move on. Leave when you are at your peak, when you've achieved what you set out to do. Don't wait until 'it's all over red rover' and people are questioning your ability to do the job. Or worse still, when you're pushed. There's nothing more demeaning or humiliating for a leader who has achieved great things to not know the right time to go – it undermines everything for which they worked so hard. Move on, find your next challenge and do great things in your next position.

And, now for the *piece de résistance*

When you have your organisation and people on-track, you've learnt to delegate and you have great teams to work with, I want you to look elsewhere. Look to where you can invest time that also gives you the same feelings of satisfaction, power and feeling valued that you get in the boardroom or from working with your people. Think of it as cross training. You will be a better, more creative leader when you put energy into and explore other areas of your life you might just have neglected for a while. Enjoy those same hot, heady feelings you've had in the boardroom but a long way away from it – you deserve it. There is no point being like my new-friend in the introduction where all she could do was to dream, hope and wish the delights would come her way.

Chapter 19 The Long & Short of it

Case studies

Merydith Willoughby wants to thank everyone who has provided a case study documenting their experience about leadership for *Sex in the Boardroom*. This generosity has made it a truly international leadership book. Some authors of case studies have chosen to be identified whilst others have not. For those who have agreed to be identified their information is detailed below. For those who prefer to remain anonymous, whilst a name appears at the end of their case study, all names, details and situations have been changed. Any resemblance to any situation or person is purely coincidental. All case studies without a name at the end of them have been written by Merydith Willoughby. All details and names in those case studies have been changed to provide anonymity.

Merydith Willoughby also wants to thank LinkedIn for providing an international business network website for professionals whereby people from all around the world can connect, ask questions and learn from each other. This website has enabled Merydith to connect with leaders all around the globe and some of these contacts have provided case studies for *Sex in the Boardroom*.

Chapter 4
Everyone's Different
Daniel Goleman, Emotional Intelligence
(New York: Bantam, 1995)

Chapter 8
Thinking
Louise Carroll, Alice's Adventures in Wonderland
(Red Queen citation)

Case Studies

Chapter 9
Continuous Improvement
Maureen Parisi
USA

Chapter 10
Keep it Simple
Domenic Cannalonga
Australia

Octavio Ballesta
Inelectra SACA
www.inelectra.com
South America

Mark F Herbert
New Paradigms LLC
www.newparadigmsllc.com
USA

Bob Stanton
www.eCern.com
USA

Bob Stewart MA
Scalar7@aol.com
USA

Chapter 18
Globalisation
Abhay Bhargava
bhargava.abhay@gmail.com
United Arab Emirates

Case Studies

Joseph Chacko
Leader
Indian Software Organisation
Mumbai

Christian Maurer
The Ultimate Sales Executive Resource
c_a_maurer@ceoexpress.com
France

Suresh Srinivasan
Microland Ltd
suresh.ss.iyer@gmail.com
India

Hamish Taylor
www.shinergise.com
United Kingdom

Serge Van Kampen
Project Manager PMP
www.linkedin.com/in/sergevankampen
Europe

Chapter 19
The Long & Short of it
Idea for cartoon
Robin Cole-Hamilton
www.massar.org.sy
Syria

Rick McElrea
Consul and Trade Commissioner
Consulate General of Canada
Sydney
Australia

Glossary of Terms

Sex in the Boardroom has been written for leaders regardless of their country of origin. Given that there are a number of terms used in the book that may be particular to Australia a Glossary of Terms has been collated.

Introduction

1. **They need the stamina of a bull and the hide of a rhinoceros:** leaders need to be able to take criticism and not unduly be affected by what others say.

2. **Whatever your reason for working with the process, know that it can assist you to be powerful beyond belief *if* and only *if* you are willing to be honest with yourself and put in the hard yards:** if leaders are willing to put in the hard work necessary to change the 'gaps' they have identified then the process in *Sex in the Boardroom* can help them to lead

powerfully. If they're not willing to do the hard work then it will have little or no positive impact on their leadership style.

3. **Some organisations realise they have to put the time and effort into developing their leaders because the so called level playing field has either gone or taken a beating with the increased competitiveness of the global market:** the term level playing field is a concept about fairness and means that not each *player* has an equal chance to succeed, but that they all play by the same set of rules.

4. **We all know the role on any given day is anything between unrelenting and exhilarating and the more endorphins you have surfing in your body – the better:** endorphins are natural compounds found in the body that can provide people with a feeling of well-being.

5. **No one wants to work with a powerful, yet cranky and unpleasant ole fart. Would *you*?** a light hearted comment which in this context relates to a leader who is powerful but has forgotten that enthusiasm, passion and fun are also important elements to being successful in their role.

Glossary of Terms

6. **They don't know how living in this pressure cooker environment for years undermines a leader being able to deliver ongoing sustainable outcomes:** working in an environment that is highly stressed.

7. **Sometimes you're on a high because everything is going so well, it all seems so effortless and then suddenly you think you're going nuts and losing the plot because things went pear shaped:** leaders generally have many things to manage and at times the role seems very easy whilst at other times their workload makes it hard to achieve necessary outcomes.

8. **Unless you implement strategies to maintain it, chinks in the armour could appear when you least expect it (or least need it) and then your once powerful leadership status might become mediocre and something you only remember in your dreams:** leaders are expected to be perfect in everything they do and they need to look after themselves if they want to continue to perform at top level.

Glossary of Terms

Chapter 1
Upline Upfront

1. **Afraid or disempowered, the incentive is to cover their backside at any cost – it is not safe to reveal themselves or to be the bearer of bad news:** it's not uncommon for employees to be too scared to tell their manager the truth because they fear recrimination.

2. **You can't afford to be kept in the dark and taken by surprise:** leaders should not assume they *know* exactly what is happening in their workplace or that they are told the truth. They need to be like private investigators at times and ask key questions of relevant people.

3. **Chris was following the 'head in the sand principle' of management, hoping that if she ignored it, it would go away and somehow fix itself:** Chris was a new manager and didn't want her manager to think she was inept, however managing the situation the way she did was likely to achieve that outcome.

4. **Your line manager bears responsibility and may be hauled over the coals for the choices you make and the information you conceal:** it is important that your workplace has a culture where managers are trusted by their people and are told the truth about what is happening in their department.

Glossary of Terms

5. **His manager isn't following the 'read my mind' model of management:** this leader needs to be upfront with his manager about the difficulties he is having as his manager can't be expected to 'fix' anything unless key information is provided.

6. **Tony knows he can face his fears and challenges, that he can enjoy having powerful people on his team and that he needs to have someone external on his side who provides him with 'another pair of eyes', support, encouragement and who is willing to ask him the tough questions that empower him to be courageous in his role:** this leader realised that by working with an executive coach he was able to gain another perspective about the same situation and then implement strategies to change what wasn't effective with his style.

7. **If you don't have all the information it's like having flat batteries in your torch: you are leading your people in the dark:** it's difficult to make decisions that impact successfully on an organisation when you haven't got all of the relevant information.

Glossary of Terms

8. **Don't assume that you are getting it because history shows clearly that it doesn't happen because fear of looking stupid affects most of us and any normal person doesn't want to put themselves in that position any more than is necessary:** most people don't want to look stupid in front of their peers or manager and may tell only parts of the whole situation to avoid being seen in this light.

Chapter 2
Square Peg

1. **At this critical juncture, if you don't manage the situation well, the culture and the rest of the team may take a hammering and your pleasant surroundings may disintegrate into bitchiness, gossiping, bullying and other unsavoury behaviours:** it is essential to manage employees who don't fit into your culture and do what is required as soon as you can because they take a lot of valuable time away from what you should be doing. They can also cause problems with other people in the workplace.

2. **We'd all love to be part of this fairy tale but odds are there's going to be some person ready to turn your world upside down:**

there are leaders who think they don't have time to assess the capability of an employee to ensure they fit into the workplace culture prior to hiring them and pay the price many times over for not doing so.

Chapter 3
Planning

1. **If planning is so important to leaders and makes such a difference to organisational success then why do so few do it and why do most of us avoid it like the plague?** planning is often considered a waste of time and avoided.

2. **You can get help, you can delegate, you can have the best people on your team but at the end of the day, it'll be your head on the plate if you don't get it right:** the leader has overall responsibility for the outcomes of their team and for mistakes that are made.

3. **It doesn't mean every day will be a bed of roses or that all targets will be met:** it means that as a leader you should not expect every day to be fantastic or that you'll always be able to do everything you'd like to do for the business. This is one of the reasons why planning and strategic management are

essential components of the role.

4. **Many things don't ever have to be done and it's fantastic to be able to look at a list and realise that a number of things can be given the flick:** regularly reviewing what you do assists you to identify those tasks that don't need to be done.

5. **Like any leader, you will wear a number of hats, so it is important to avoid taking on so much that you are unable to achieve your desired outcomes:** leaders have many responsibilities and need to be aware of what they agree to do. Saying yes to too many things may mean that you are unable to do any one thing properly.

6. **If this process is likely to be put in the too hard basket then get someone to work with you and to teach you how to do it:** if this process is something you don't know how to do and you are likely not to do it then find someone who can help you learn these skills.

7. **Good planning does not guarantee smooth sailing but once leaders see what a huge difference it makes they wonder why they didn't commit to the process earlier:** whilst

good planning is unable to guarantee that everything will go according to plan it is a wise manager who knows the benefit of doing it.

8. **Without planning you're just adrift hoping that things will go right and determinedly ignoring the fact that you may well wash up somewhere you don't want to be:** not planning effectively could mean that you end up not achieving necessary organisational goals and that you spend a lot of time *hoping* things will go okay for the business.

9. **You and those you lead waste much less time on activities that are not adding value to your business, fire fighting in problem areas and being caught in dramas:** people in management learn the art of delegation and stop doing what won't bring them the results they need to achieve organisational goals.

Chapter 4
Everyone's Different

1. **Although we have a modus operandi and sometimes slip into the assumption that everyone thinks like us, as leaders we must see through this:** human beings are all individuals and have their own thought

processes. Leaders should not assume that their people think the same way they do.

2. **Well, armed with this information, we as leaders get insights into human behaviour and can learn how to get the best out of those we lead:** effective leadership requires understanding as to how to get the maximum out of your people.

3. **There will be some employees who are very easy to get on with and there will be some who drive you crazy because they seem to put a spanner in the works at every step:** some employees are a pleasure to work with whilst others seem to make it deliberately hard for you to do your role effectively. Often leaders allow the difficult employees to take up far too much of their valuable time which means they don't have time for other necessary things. Balance is important here and being aware as to just how much time you're investing into people who do not help you to achieve business outcomes is essential. Do an inventory on this regularly.

4. **When the situation blew up an hour into the afternoon manager's shift, he was annoyed**

and embarrassed to be in the dark about a serious safety breach and thought that any disciplinary action the employee got would be richly deserved: a manager who knew nothing about a situation that had occurred in an earlier shift had to manage it.

5. **Concerned that an employee with a good record had placed himself in a difficult position, the manager telephoned him at home and strongly advised him to report back to work and make a clean breast of the situation:** the manager encouraged the employee to take full responsibility for what had occurred and to write a report.

6. **During the conversation it became clear that the employee had been badly rattled by what happened and had gone home without saying anything simply because he didn't know what to do and was afraid of the consequences:** the employee was upset by the situation that occurred and didn't know how to handle the situation.

Chapter 5
Performance

1. **This is not rocket science:** the process is basic business practice and shouldn't be hard

to understand.

2. **Your program need not cost a squillion dollars:** performance management tools do not have to cost your organisation significant sums of money.

3. **You don't have a commitment to micro management unless it's necessary and then it's only for that period to get the person up to scratch:** managers use micro management as a tool to assist those who need it to become high performers. Once achieved they then allow them more leeway.

4. **Would you know what they thought or would they present you with a smile and belittle you afterwards?** an employee is agreeable whilst the person is around but vindictive when they leave.

5. **All of the above would generally be with the best of intentions but you know what the way to hell is paved with, don't you?** many employees think they are doing the best for the organisation whereas what they are doing is not conducive to increasing organisational strength.

6. **You stop bashing your head against a brick wall and instead you walk the talk:** you stop doing what doesn't work and find solutions to the issues you are facing.

7. **Are the results used to acknowledge what your people have done well or to lambaste them for what they haven't achieved?** does the manager acknowledge the employee for what they have done well or use the information to be nasty to the person involved.

Chapter 6
Your Style

1. **If you are able to nail your look and have a fantastic style, it will make a huge difference to you and the way you operate:** you develop your personal powerful style.

2. **Even if someone says you were fantastic, be aware that you might have been dead boring:** be aware that not everyone will tell you the truth about the way you present and you need to surround yourself with people who will tell you as it really is.

3. **Keep up-to-date with what's happening in this area for your own sake because you**

don't want to be considered an old fossil: as a leader you don't want to be considered old fashioned and unaware of current trends.

Chapter 7
Workplace Culture

1. **They don't have an *I'm better than those plebs* attitude:** senior management treat all of their people with respect and get to know them.

2. **It takes a lot out of them to do this because they already have enough on their plate but they want to do it because they like their people, they employed them and these are the people that help them to achieve the organisation's ongoing success:** it may cause managers stress to do this because they already have enough work to do.

3. **Instead of throwing in the towel, she decided to apply for her job:** the manager didn't leave the organisation when having to apply for their own position because of the commitment they felt to their people.

4. **Take your eye off the ball for a while and it could take you a long time to get back to where you were:** leaders need to remain focused.

Chapter 8
Thinking

1. **And if one of your people says it's all fantastic, that is your cue to do a bit of mining and find out what is really going on:** ask relevant questions to find out what is not being said.

Chapter 9
Continuous Improvement

1. **It means that anyone who has anything to do with the organisation is on the same page: management, employees and all stakeholders:** every stakeholder knows exactly what is expected of them.

2. **They constantly review, keeping their eye on the ball, remembering their objectives and the outcomes that they need to achieve each time they are in the cockpit of their aircraft:** the person in charge knows what they are doing and is focused on achieving necessary outcomes.

3. **Staff had been informed yet again that they had to make budgetary cuts and so they just slashed and burned to get the figures right:** budgetary cuts were required and changes were made to the organisation that were not conducive to increasing productivity.

4. **He learnt that he needed to stop his happy chappy approach and stop doing everything for his team when they were quite capable of doing it for themselves given they'd all been there a lot longer than he had:** a manager was too friendly with his staff and not doing what he was paid to do.

5. **Lewis had felt horrible, as if he was losing the plot and didn't have a clue how to handle his seemingly wayward staff:** the leader felt as though whatever he did was ineffective with his team and he had to learn how to manage them.

6. **Not every idea will end up being implemented or viable but it will help more people become 'thinkers in residence' and to have continuous improvement embedded in your culture:** leaders can assist their people to think about what they're doing and to improve their systems and processes.

Chapter 10
Keep it Simple

1. **Worrying about covering our backside rather than making the right decision:** this relates to making a decision that is not in the best interest of the business but protects the person involved.

2. **Pushing people harder than they thought they could perform and making sure they knew I had their back covered:** the executive provided his staff with support and through this encouragement they achieved great things.

3. **I relate that somewhat tongue in cheek, but how much time do we spend on piddly issues?** at times those in leadership can focus on issues that are not important instead of looking at successful outcomes being achieved.

4. **Having their personal weekly meeting can make the difference between years of head banging experiences and getting ahead, learning what needs to be done, doing it, identifying what needs tweaking and then tweaking it:** leaders have found that being committed to their personal weekly meeting assists them to stop wasting time on peripheral issues.

Chapter 11
Meetings

1. **However, they can be an over-used time wasting exercise with leaders racing mindlessly from one meeting to another**

without having time to prepare for the meeting or to assess whether they are of benefit: it's not uncommon for business to have meetings just because it's what they've always done. Meetings take a lot of time, they take people away from other duties and participants need to ensure they prepare adequately for them otherwise they're just a waste of time and money and provide no real benefit to the organisation.

2. **She has been railroading about a particular project just recently, expecting me to let her have her own way:** this business partner is determined to do what they want. She bullies the rest of the team into what she wants under the guise of being democratic.

Chapter 12
Stress

1. **The invincibility of our adolescent years is still with us and even though we hear about what it can do to people and see others fall by the wayside we doggedly resist accepting that it could happen to us:** this refers to those leaders who believe they can work excessive hours, not take holidays, be connected to their mobile and email 24x7 and firmly believe that

stress will not impact on the way they lead their people or on their health.

Chapter 13
Ignorance is Bliss

1. **When leaders do the *dig* they realise that ignorance isn't bliss:** leaders realise that it is better to know what's *really* happening in the workplace rather than to kid themselves that all is well.

2. **It takes them awhile to realise and to accept that it's okay to acknowledge themselves for what they do rather than beat up on themself over the occasional occurrence that didn't go the way they intended:** there are many fine leaders who are always striving to improve themselves, their systems and processes and who genuinely care about those they lead. They also achieve great things for their employer. Often these same leaders are their own harshest critic.

3. **One mistake and they will hammer themselves for days but their many successes won't be enjoyed for even one second:** the leader focuses on what they haven't done well rather than to acknowledge the outstanding results they have achieved. They generally deflect compliments.

Glossary of Terms

4. **What was clear to the other directors and staff was that this person worked tirelessly for the CEO, smiled when he was around, couldn't do enough for him but the moment his back was turned she belittled him:** a subordinate was friendly to her leader's face and spoke disparagingly about him when he wasn't there.

5. **And she still does exactly the same as she's always done – is nasty behind his back and to his face is lovely, kind and acts like the person you would want in your life as a best friend, colleague and support:** the employee lambastes the person behind their back.

Chapter 14
Fear

1. **Like bullying, it often gets swept under the carpet:** stress is often considered a *soft* issue in business and leaders are expected to just get on with it. There is enough research to show quite clearly that stress has a huge impact on leaders and these studies need to be accepted and addressed in the workplace.

Chapter 15
Fake it until You make it

1. **As such, you are expected to be perfect, no chinks in your armour, perfect in everything that you do, able to work continuously and not be fatigued, the magician who is able to pull rabbits out of hats time and time again, more powerful than a locomotive and able to leap tall buildings in a single bound:** in general, society and business have unrealistic expectations of leaders and they are expected to achieve far more than anyone really can.

2. **Once he did that, he started soaring with the eagles and loved it:** the leader became confident and successful.

3. **It is never easy taking someone on and explaining to them why their behaviour is unacceptable:** it can take a lot of courage to speak to someone who has treated you badly.

4. **And when you need to change tack you do it seamlessly because you can:** the speaker is aware of their audience and gives them what they want.

Glossary of Terms

5. **Naomi could have fallen in a heap:** Naomi could have given up and started apologising for what was happening and accepted responsibility for things that she had no control over. Rather than allow the situation to dominate she delivered the best performance she could under the circumstances.

Chapter 16
Bullying

1. **Try using different words to avoid getting their back up but don't allow their aggression to dominate you or to stop you from doing what you have to do:** don't allow someone's aggression to stop you from doing what is required of you as a leader when bullying is occurring in the workplace.

2. **Then to cap it off, we changed the strategic plan because the one that was in place when I started really wasn't going to work:** the manager denied the employee what was rightly theirs.

3. **Most bullies roll over when they are brought to justice and just like dogs, want their belly scratched:** whilst bullies appear to be powerful in reality most of them have low self-esteem.

Glossary of Terms

4. **After 'the final straw' had occurred and the manager said one nasty thing too many, Leeane let her know clearly that she didn't like the way she was being treated and she needed to treat herwithrespect:** theemployee involved had had enough of being treated badly and decided to inform the manager that their behaviour was unacceptable.

5. **Let your people know that whilst you aren't perfect you will do your utmost to stomp on bullying as soon as you become aware that it is happening:** advise your people that bullying is not tolerated in the workplace.

Chapter 18
Globalisation

1. **If you go in with an arrogant attitude, they'll be ready to enjoy the spectacle of you coming unstuck:** leaders need to be aware of their attitude to ensure they are not unintentionally alienating their staff.

2. **So be patient and tolerant, be understanding of differences and willing to go that extra mile for your people:** when leaders are managing people in other countries they need to be willing to educate themselves properly

about the way things are done in that country rather than impose their own idealist view.

Chapter 19
The Long & Short of it

1. **Pushing yourself too hard won't achieve powerful results because anyone who works themselves to the bone performs below par in the long run:** powerful leadership doesn't mean you have to work 24x7. It means that you take care of yourself because you know ultimately by doing so will lead to better outcomes for you and those you lead.

2. **Don't wait until 'it's all over red rover' and people are questioning your ability to do the job:** it's sad to see leaders who have achieved great things in their current role to stay on for too long. This generally occurs because they are passionate about what they do and they don't realise that their time has past and they should be looking for other employment opportunities.

www.ingramcontent.com/pod-product-compliance
Lightning Source LLC
Chambersburg PA
CBHW071858290426
44110CB00013B/1190